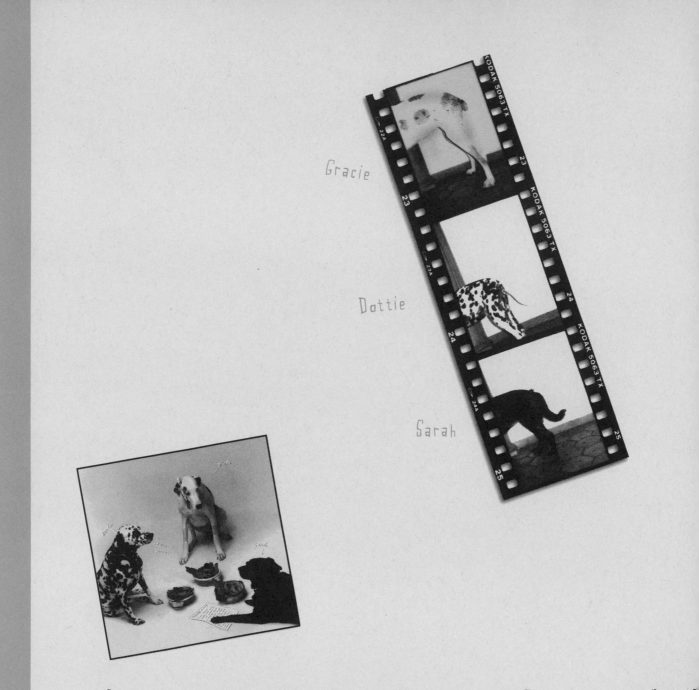

Gracie

Dottie

Sarah

A Canine Compendium Full of Pawsitively Scrumptious Top S

Short Tails And Treats
from
Three Dog Bakery

Dan Dye and Mark Beckloff

Andrews and McMeel
A Universal Press Syndicate Company
Kansas City

et Recipes, Anecdogs and Never-Before-Seen Photographs!

Handlettered typeface, Meg Condensed, © Meg Cundiff, 1996
Illustrated by Meg Cundiff
Typeset by Randall Blair

Graphic on p. 82 reprinted by permission of *The Wall Street Journal* © 1993 Dow Jones & Company, Inc. All Rights Reserved Worldwide.

Happy Days Are Here Again, by Jack Yellen and Milton Ager © 1929 (Renewed) Warner Bros. Inc.; All Rights Reserved; Used By Permission
WARNER BROS. PUBLICATIONS U.S. INC., Miami, FL. 33014

Photographer Credits
Tim Pott: p. 1, 6, 11, 12, 14, 17, 75, 77, 83, 102, 109, 111; Tatjana Alvegaard: p. 7, 113; Humberto Ramirez: p. 2, 63, 68, 84; Meg Cundiff: p. 2, 98, 112; Dan Dye: p. 3, 16, 108; Theresa Heim: p. 64; LuAnn Beckloff: p. 99

Library of Congress Cataloging-in-Publication Data:

Dye, Dan
  Short tails and treats from Three Dog Bakery / Dan Dye and Mark Beckloff.
        p.   cm.
  ISBN 0-8362-2155-9 (pbk.)
  1. Three Dog Bakery (Kansas City, MO)--History. 2. Dogs--Food--Miscellanea.
I. Beckloff, Mark II. Three Dog Bakery (Kansas City, Mo.) III. Title.
HD9340.U54T483   1996
381' .4566466'09778411--dc20

96-30923
CIP

Attention: Schools and Businesses

Contents

This book is dedicated
to all dogs everywhere
and to all the people
who love them.

Chapter 1

WE LOVE DOGS!
AND DOGS LOVE US!

Hello. And a big, fat, juicy, wet, slobbery lick on the face to you for buying our book. If this is your introduction to our bakery, WELCOME and come on in! If you are already a customer or already know of us, THANK YOU. We appreciate it!

Our names are Daniel Dye and Mark Beckloff and we are the founders and owners of Kansas City's famed Three Dog Bakery, The Bakery For Dogs. This is our own wags-to-riches story of how we came to start the world's most unique bakery—a bone-ified, five-paw bakery—for dogs. Ours is a Canine Confectionery, a Pooch Patisserie, a Mecca For Mutts where dogs go to see and be seen, nibble and be nibbled, sniff and be sniffed. Three Dog Bakery is our humble shrine to the magnanimous, mutt-umental mongrel spirit.

We are also the proud owners of Sarah Jean (an eight-year-old Black Lab mix), Dottie Louise (a seven-year-old Dalmatian) and Gracie Marie (our big six-year-old Great Dane baby), Three Dog Bakery's founding sisters. When they are not busy eating all the profits, they can be found serving the company in many ways including, but not limited to: Quality Control

Supervisors, Taste Test Engineers, Official Front Door Greeters and UPS Delivery Man Growlers. They have become quite famous in their own right …their pictures gracing the pages of our nation's magazines, their images splashed on television screens and in newspapers the world over. But they have still managed to retain their humble mutt, small-town friendliness and natural, unspoiled charm and modesty. Well, sort of. More about the girls later.

As you might well imagine, oddball questions go hand-in-paw with owning a bakery for dogs. "Can you make a goat's milk biscuit?" (We could.) "You don't use real kittens in the Big Scary Kitties, do you?" (Just for the record, we don't.) One recurring area of interest is, "Why on earth did you start a bakery for dogs? What gave you the idea?"

The answer is simple: **WE LOVE DOGS!** We truly do. Silly, hyper, short, grumpy, loud, wild or shy, we love 'em all. For some crazy reason, dogs just give us the biggest kick. We both desperately wanted to quit our "real" jobs, to be unleashed from the corporate dog-eat-dog world, but we had no idea what to do. For months we tossed all sorts of ideas around. We knew we had to center our potential business around something that we genuinely loved and would not grow resentful toward if we had to start working at it twenty-four hours a day. The more we thought about it, the more we knew our idea had to have something to do with dogs. Then, as you will soon read, we determined there was a genuine void in the marketplace for wholesome, all-natural, fresh-baked dog treats. This became our selling niche and our company, **KC-K9 Bakery, Inc.,** was conceived in the final days of 1989.

Customers often comment on how lucky we are to be doing what we do. And of course, they are absolutely right. We are blessed—and I mean *truly,*

Perky

Pensive

Shy

Silly

Short

grumpy

8

extraordinarily blessed—to make our living doing something we love and to which we feel a total commitment. Every time we hear someone complaining about their job, we are reminded of just how lucky we are.

However, we would be lying if we did not reveal that there were many, many long, hard days and nights of hand-kneading stiff biscuit dough for our next day's orders. We worked like dogs! And we went home dog-tired! Our first few years were filled with day after endless day of relentless, wrist-throbbing, mind-numbing, lift-that-barge-tote-that-bale, dough-kneading.

Then, to add to our biscuit-baking enjoyment, every dime of our money went back into the business to keep it operating. It seemed like every day was a God-I-Hope-Some-Checks-Come-In-Today kind of day. We became mas-

POWER & LIGHT MAN

CHEESE TWISTS

ZAP'S FAVORITE Lights-out TREAT

, the Power and Light guy's dog

2 cups whole wheat flour
1/4 cup cornmeal
1/2 cup Parmesan cheese

1 medium egg
3/4 cup water

Preheat oven to 325 degrees. Combine all ingredients except 1/4 cup Parmesan cheese. Knead until thoroughly mixed. Using a teaspoon, scoop out dough and roll into quarter-size balls. On a lightly floured surface, roll balls into pencil-shaped "sticks" in extra Parmesan cheese until sticks are coated. Flatten with rolling pin or by hand. Twist each stick 6-8 times and place on an ungreased baking sheet. Bake approximately 30 minutes. Cool on pan. Store in sealed container. Yield: 18 sticks.

ters *paw excellence* of robbing Peter to pay Paul. There was more than one occasion when the light at the end of the tunnel turned out to be the headlights of the Power and Light truck, coming to shut off our electricity.

Luckily, we both were driven by a shared, inspired vision: **to create the best dog treats in the world.** Thank God, ignorance truly *is* bliss, and because of our stupidity—or our brilliance—we were able to keep each other motivated. That's why we are total advocates of partnerships in business. The moral, I guess, is that there is always a flip side to every so-called success story. Our advice to you (not that you asked) is: follow your heart—really *honestly* follow your passion—and success will unfold itself around you in ways you cannot even imagine.

But getting back to dogs: neither of us can recall life without dogs. As kids, we played and ran for hours on end with our dog(s). There was never a time when our families did not each have at least one dog. I remember, when I was four, Lassie, our collie (hey! now there's an original name), biting me in the face for introducing him to a stray cat I was carrying. And growing up with Blue, who became Ol' Blue as she ran, walked, then hobbled her sweet way through nearly twenty years of life. And Fred, the wigglebutt boxer who would smother you with kisses for just looking at him.

Even today, as we observe dogs through adult eyes, we still marvel at them. In fact, lately we have come to appreciate dogs for yet another reason: the incredible lessons about life and about ourselves that dogs can teach us, if we are only willing to listen. Start by just studying your dogs. Pay close attention to the joy in which they live their lives, the happiness they find in the smallest details. Watch the next time he or she wakes up. It doesn't matter if it's 6:00 A.M. or midnight . . . they just **WAKE UP!** And **POW!** Just like that! They're ready for life's next adventure. There is something so great about that. We are usually so busy scurrying around being humanoids that we hardly ever stop long enough to even notice life's small, everyday delights.

Sometimes I silently watch Sarah, Dottie and Gracie as they mill around in the morning, impatiently waiting to go to work. As we leave the house and I open my truck's door, they hop in, one by one. For all they know, we could be heading out for a ten-year excursion through China. They couldn't care less. They just seem so happy to be alive. Dogs live so in-the-moment. No worries. No gnawing self-doubts. No lingering feelings of inadequacy. Just pure, honest, simple life-enjoyment. What a way to live! What lessons our dogs can teach us!

At this point, we would be remiss and severely chastised if we did not introduce the three naughty girls for whom our bakery is named. Their pawsitive spirits, fetching good looks and love of a good bone (not necessarily in that order) have helped us to create our unique concept. **First we have**

11

The Enchanting Miss Sarah Jean

Sarah Jean, the Biscuit Queen, is a sweetie-pie eight-year-old Black Lab mix who grins when she's very happy. She was adopted from one of the city's animal shelters when she was just a wee, shy, butterball puppy. She is always very funny and always in a great mood. She is extremely smart and incredibly eager to please. Sarah is the one who will rise out of a cozy, sound sleep to investigate the smallest rustling of a sound. She feels that it is her duty to protect us. I appreciate that about her.

It is said that adopted puppies from the pound make the best pets and we believe that to be true. They never forget the scary loneliness of their incarceration. Imagine not knowing who can be trusted and who should be feared. **Let it be known far and wide that Three Dog Bakery warmly salutes all pet owners who adopt their pets from the pound or take in strays. People who save animals are true heroes in our eyes.**

Sarah quickly became the apple of our eyes and the center of the entire known universe. Furry squeaky toys, leashes, outgrown collars, rawhides and dog hair soon blanketed the house. Every day was a new opportunity for Sarah to seek out and destroy our meager possessions. Yet every morning as I left for work and said good-bye to Sarah, a twinge of guilt would shadow over me. "Poor little thing," I'd think, gazing down into her sad, mournful eyes. "She needs a baby sister to keep her company."

Imagine our joy, when just six months after Sarah's arrival, the stork brought a new bundle of joy:

Sarah Jean's Crowning Crumpets

WHEN the QUEEN Demands the BEST!

2 cups cornmeal
I cup cake flour
2 tablespoons vegetable oil
I egg
2/3 cup honey

1 1/3 cups water
1/2 teaspoon baking powder
1/4 cup real bacon bits
Paper baking cups

Preheat oven to 350 degrees. Mix all ingredients together. Spoon into muffin pan lined with paper baking cups. Bake for approximately 40 to 45 minutes. Cool.

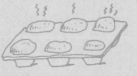

The Beguiling Miss Dottie Louise

Dottie, the Ever-Expanding, is a seven-year-old Dalmatian who will eat anything that doesn't eat her first. Literally. When she first came home she was a cuddly, spotty little ball of fur. Her little round eyes were still puppy-blue. She had to have been the most energetic, mischievous, happy, rambunctious puppy who ever lived. At one point, in desperation, we were actually considering starting a support group for Dalmatian puppy owners.

We are exhaustedly happy to report that Dottie has matured—finally—into a refined, dignified, gentle, tail-wagging snuggle-bug. Looking into Dottie's calm, serene, little face today, it is hard to imagine that there once raged a godless pagan, a holy terror of a beast. Marauding, plundering, pillaging, destroying, looting and consuming any obstacle foolish enough to dare cross her path of debauchery and mayhem.

Dottie is further proof that girls truly do just want to have fun. She lives for the next adventure, the thrill of the hunt. Nothing is more satisfying to Dottie than stalking prey. **Dottie the Warrior!** Birds, butterflies, squirrels and rabbits…woe be to the unfortunate critter that enters Dottie's backyard domain. Of course, 99.9 percent of the time, she fails miserably to capture her intended victim, but I'm sure in her mind she believes that she has left nothing but grisly remains on the lawn. **Dottie the Mighty! Dottie the Fierce!**

When we first brought Dottie home, Sarah seemed upset . . . for at least fifteen minutes. Within an hour, they were frolicking through the house and the yard and back into the house again. After several hours of exhausting play, it became strangely quiet. I peeked out the back door and saw them asleep on the porch, Dottie curled up and nestled in between her new big sister's paws. Sarah and Dottie have been literally inseparable ever since.

By the time we got Dottie, Sarah was already pretty well on her way to being trained. So she really helped

Dottie's Banana Biscotti

JUST Add SOME RAISINS TO MAKE them SPOTTIE...LIKE ME!

5 cups white flour
1/4 cup peanuts, chopped
1/2 teaspoon baking soda
1 medium egg

1/4 cup vegetable oil
1 1/2 cups banana (pureed)
2 teaspoons pure vanilla
Water

Preheat oven to 325 degrees. Mix dry, then wet ingredients until lumpy. Add water one teaspoon at a time as needed. Knead by hand on table until mixed thoroughly. Form into logs approximately 2 to 2 1/2 inches high. Flatten so that log is 6 to 7 inches wide by 1 inch high. Place on nonstick baking sheets. Bake for approximately 30 to 40 minutes. Remove and cool 10 minutes. Slice into 1/2- to 3/4-inch slices. Place on baking sheets and bake for approximately 20 minutes or until golden brown. Cool, serve!

in training Dottie, since Dottie just mimicked what she saw Sarah do. In mere days, Dottie was potty-trained, able to shake, sit and sneak food off of the kitchen counters. After another six months went by, we reflected on the fact that two dogs were hardly more trouble than one. So, as dog lovers are prone to do, we rationalized that a third dog wouldn't be—*couldn't be*—that much more trouble. Boy were we ever **WRONG!**

A friend of ours had just gotten a very cute Great Dane puppy, whom she named Merlin. She slyly revealed that there was one more puppy left in the litter and urged us to go look at her. Eventually, after about a minute and a half, our resistance to her hypnotic suggestions completely wore down and we agreed to go look at her.

HER MOST SERENE ROYAL MAJESTY GRACIE MARIE

Gracie is a gigantic, huge, enormous, dinosaur-sized, beautiful, lovable Great Dane. She is an albino, so she has mostly white coloring, with beautiful Paul Newman baby blue eyes. She was born stone deaf and that has made her even more precious to us. Gracie is very, very shy and humble in the most cuddly sort of way. She honestly has no concept of how big she really is. To her mind, she is no bigger than a dainty little Chihuahua.

Not long ago, I watched Gracie as something caught her attention. She got up with that wrinkled-forehead, curious-face that Great Danes wear and lumbered over to the middle of the floor. She stared, then pawed at the floors, her inch-long toenails gouging out vast crevices into the hardwood planks (thanks, Gracie) and began to act frisky. She growled playfully and pawed the floor again and again. I had to look very carefully to determine that her playmate was (key word being WAS) a ladybug. I'm sure Gracie thought she was an equal match for her new friend.

And she is the biggest baby. She loves to take her toys to bed with her and sleep under the covers. She also hides when someone comes to the door and peeks around corners until she determines it's OK to come out.

Gracie is irresistibly adorable and is a great conversation piece as well. One of the most frequently asked questions at the bakery is, "What kind of horse is that?" Since her ears are not cropped and she's so white with blue eyes, she just looks, well, odd. But in a very beautiful, exotic sort of way.

Sarah and Dottie were not exactly thrilled when Gracie arrived. For one thing, they could sense something seemed wrong with her. She didn't wake up to greet us when we got home from work, since she was deaf. All the

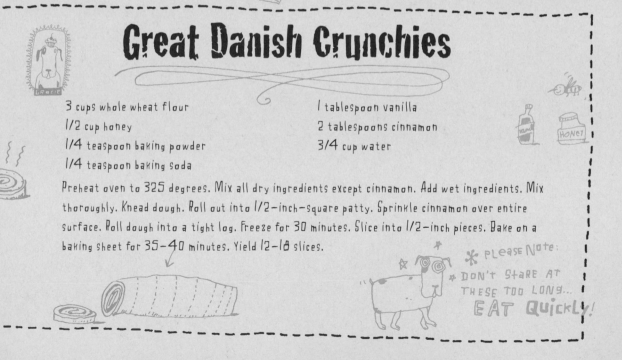

Great Danish Crunchies

3 cups whole wheat flour
1/2 cup honey
1/4 teaspoon baking powder
1/4 teaspoon baking soda

1 tablespoon vanilla
2 tablespoons cinnamon
3/4 cup water

Preheat oven to 325 degrees. Mix all dry ingredients except cinnamon. Add wet ingredients. Mix thoroughly. Knead dough. Roll out into 1/2-inch-square patty. Sprinkle cinnamon over entire surface. Roll dough into a tight log. Freeze for 30 minutes. Slice into 1/2-inch pieces. Bake on a baking sheet for 35-40 minutes. Yield 12-18 slices.

* PLEASE NOTE:
* DON'T STARE AT THESE TOO LONG...
EAT QUICKLY!

audio cues that revolve through a hearing dog's day went unnoticed by Gracie and they thought that was weird. Plus, now the pack order was all mixed up. The girls whipped themselves into a frenzy on who would be the alpha dog and so on. Of course, Sarah Smartypants won that contest.

To be quite honest, both Sarah and Dottie were absolute snots to Gracie for the longest time. But then, Gracie began to grow, as Great Danes have a tendency to do, and they were obliged to grudgingly show her a bit more respect. When we first got Gracie she could walk underneath Sarah's belly without even touching. However, she seemed to quadruple in size each week for a year and a half. We can still remember Sarah and Dottie trembling in horror as they watched Gracie grow and grow and grow and grow. "My God! Will she ever stop?" they seemed to ask us with their eyes.

Finally Gracie did stop growing and today the three girls are the best of friends. Although with three hundred pounds' worth of dogs tearing through the house at any given time, we have long since given up on trying to have nice things. Mom *was* right: we *can't* have nice things. But it's worth it. We can't imagine life any other way. The joy that our dogs bring to us far outweighs the fact that we don't have a fancy sofa. Who cares! So what! You can't take it with you . . . which is another life lesson that dogs seem to understand better than we do.

We hope you have enjoyed getting to know the girls and us a little better. We are now ready to em-bark on the adventurous journey of how we came to start Three Dog Bakery, soon to be famous the world rover!

Chapter 2

A Bare Bones Beginning

It's so hard to believe that it's been over forty years since we started Three Dog Bakery. Well, that would be in dog years. In human terms, it has been just about six years since we burnt our first biscuit. What an incredible journey we've had! What incredible people we've met! What great dogs have sniffed their way into our lives.

Our story began during a bitterly cold Kansas City Christmas way back in 19 and 89. Knowing how much Mark loved his dogs, his mom, LuAnn, put a dog biscuit recipe and dog bone cookie cutter in his Christmas stocking. She thought it would make a great stocking stuffer. Boy, did it ever. Immediately, a bright, blinding light bulb went off over both our heads. DOG BISCUITS! FRESH-BAKED DOG BISCUITS! WE LOVE DOGS!

At long last, we knew what we could do to give meaning to our pathetic, empty lives: we would start baking the best, tastiest dog biscuits in the world! I know it sounds like an oversimplification to say the idea hit us that quickly, but it did. We had been desperately—do you hear me?—**desperately** searching for the right idea, the big one, which would enable us to quit our real jobs. And in that brief, shining moment, that beautiful, sweet, triumphant moment, the vision roared over us like a 250-pound bullmastiff. **We would commence, immediately, to bake the best dog biscuit the civilized world had ever known.**

We became giddy with enthusiasm as we began to rationalize why our idea was a great one. In fact, the more we discussed our new venture, the more excited we became. After years of purchasing store-bought, commercially available biscuits for our own various dogs, we felt we were at least marginally entitled to demand better. Let's face it: dog treats were boring. And sometimes just plain creepy.

It was easy for us to visualize a great, wholesome, fresh-baked biscuit, using only tasty, simple, close-to-the-earth ingredients. We thought it was amazing that there was nothing like this on the market. Could this be our niche? We already knew, based on a lifetime of informal observations, that dogs drastically preferred the flavors of honey and whole wheat over sodium benzoate any day of the week.

So what was the deal? How could we explain to Sarah, Dottie and Gracie that the treats they were eating had a longer shelf life than *they* did?

We began to explore the dog treat sections of the local supermarkets and pet stores. Like two rat terriers stalking our prey, we sniffed through aisle after aisle reading ingredient labels. What we read curled our hair tighter than a poodle's. Not only were dog treats boring, which was the ultimate crime, they were also filled with scary sounding chemical additives and preservatives. Artificial, quasi-foodstuffs developed in laboratories by sinister-looking guys in white jackets. What could possibly be the point of adding fifty ingredients to a simple dog treat? Especially when we couldn't even pronounce forty of those ingredients, let alone know why they were there. Adding chemicals simply to prolong shelf life just wasn't a strong-enough argument.

I remembered something that had happened when I was moving out of my dad's house after college. Finally on my own, free to live the life I was bone to lead: that of a wild, hot, unneutered stud. As I packed up my worldly possessions, I came across a box of biscuits buried deep in a dresser drawer. Oddly enough, I could completely recall purchasing the treats— *some five years earlier*—as a reward for Blue, my good ol' dog. As I opened the box, I wondered why I had stuck them in my dresser drawer. What makes this story so weird is that even after five years, the biscuits smelled the same, looked the same and for all practical (or impractical) purposes **were** the same as the day they were purchased. That story is a perfect example of why we started our company. There had to be a better way.

THE EXACT SAME
dog BisCuit

1982

1987

So every day we'd come home from work, eager to begin fantasizing again about our dog bone emporium. What a perfect idea! We began to compile lists of ingredients, names of veterinarians, pet stores and other useful information. The next time the girls went for a checkup, we asked the vet probing questions about nutritional information that proved invaluable. We called other vets and vet schools. Our next step was to actually begin baking. Never mind that we had no baking experience. We'd cross that bridge when we came to it.

Keep in mind we had no money whatsoever. Like most other good, old-fashioned, red-blooded Americans, we always made sure that we spent more than we made. One important note: this is not a good way to start a business. But the good news was we had unbridled enthusiasm for our new project which, as it turned out, was every bit as helpful as having a large bank account. We also had a passion for dogs, which became our guiding light through our start-up operation.

So after a few months of scheming and dreaming and blatant procrastination, we finally cleared off the kitchen counters one Saturday morning and officially started our new biscuiteria: **KC-K9 Bakery**. We had toyed with different names and came up with several that we really liked. But being from Kansas City and loving canines the way we did, we decided the name **KC-K9** seemed a natural, logical choice. We proudly stood by our name for our first four years of business and still fondly recall the utter simplicity of our early days. But as we began to expand into other cities, we discovered that Kansas City was not the center of the universe as we had been led to believe and some people did not understand what our name meant.

We used to get a lot of calls asking if we trained guard dogs. Not exactly the image we were hoping to evoke. Then we began to discover, much to our dismay, that the directory assistance operators were unable to locate our name for our out-of-town customers. They would look under Casey Canine, KCK Nine, KayCee K9, you name it . . . everything but KC-K9. In November 1994, before we got any bigger, we determined that it was time to change our name to one that people could understand and thus became **Three Dog Bakery—The Bakery For Dogs.**

As you can well imagine, this new name made the three girls extremely happy. They had been worried that somehow, in the excitement, they would be left out. In fact, the only way they could have been happier would have been if we had named the bakery specifically after one of them. Sarah schemed about **"Sarah's Snack Shack,"** Dottie dreamed of **"Dottie's Delicious Delicacies"** and Gracie gravitated toward **"Gracie's Gracious Goodies."** So the new name was a nice compromise.

Back to our start: we had gone to our neighborhood's health food store the night before and purchased flour, wheat germ, spinach, carrots and all the other ingredients we were going to mix in. We already had the wooden spoon, mixing bowl and two baking pans. Our house is located in one of the oldest neighborhoods in Kansas City and in it stood what was surely one of the oldest ovens as well. It was (and *is*— we still use it) an old 1930s Chambers oven and I'm sure in its day it was quite the appliance. After the biscuits were rolled out and cut one by one, I lit the pilot light with a match and we were on our way. . . .

The first problem we encountered was the size of the oven's actual cooking chamber. It was so small! Each baking tray would hold only 1 3/4 pounds of biscuits and the oven would cook only two trays at a time. That's only 3 1/2 pounds of biscuits per cooking cycle. Our Great Dane, Gracie, was looking a bit apprehensive. Would we be able to bake fast enough to satisfy her goodie-loving appetite? Would we be able to fulfill her dreams of a never-ending biscuit supply? The air was thick with tension.

We carefully monitored the oven and opened the door every five minutes to peer in. I wish I could report that our first batch was a howling success, but, alas, we had to chalk it up to experience. Same with the second batch.

FLOUR X
WHEAT GERM X
SPINACH X
CARROTS X
RAISINS
OATS X
CAROB CHIPS X

And third. Biscuit baking was going to be a bit harder than we had thought. By the end of the day, we were wondering what in the heck we were doing wrong. After carefully cooling our disasters, er, biscuits, we would lay them on the counter for an inspection. Some were too dark, others too light. Some too hard, others were curled or bubbled.

But the taste? How was the flavor? We nearly broke our teeth biting into those first flops. But hmmmm. Actually, they were not too bad tasting. However we were not the true judges. We lined up several of the biscuits on the floor and watched with a scientist's precision the girl's reactions. As if to offer us moral support, Sarah, Dottie and Gracie cautiously sniffed then immediately munched and crunched their way through several pounds of treats. However, their faces betrayed them. Their faces seemed to say, "Thanks for the attempt, and we appreciate your efforts, but what is this? Please get a clue!" Of course Dottie, ever appreciative of any offered tidbit, thought the burnt ones were done cajun style . . . Blackened Biscuits.

That evening, we sat down together to rehash our first day's baking experience. We both offered up our own explanations of what we were doing wrong and what we could do to make the biscuits perfect. Was it too much oil? Not enough? Oven too hot? Not hot enough? More water? Less beef broth? **WHAT WERE WE DOING WRONG?** I'm sure a baking expert—even any grandma worth her salt—could have come in and said, "Stand back, ninnies, while I show you how to bake a biscuit!" But, no, that would have been too easy. We had to figure it out ourselves.

The next day we awoke refreshed and more determined than ever to discover the error of our ways. Once again, we mixed, kneaded, preheated, poked, prodded, burnt, cussed and discussed. Once again the girls were asked to sample our wares, they grudgingly obliged. Except, again, for spotty little Dottie who ravenously consumed any morsel of food which came within striking distance. A precious weekend was over, wasted, and all we had to show for it were aching limbs and a cookie jar filled with bone-shaped, dark, rock-hard objects. Sarah, sensing our disappointment, nestled in ever closer on the couch that night, her sweet little face and big, brown eyes saying, "Losers."

We knew there was still hope. We couldn't give in. I knew I was quite the grillmeister at the barbecue pit. And who else but Mark could bake such a mean lasagna? There had to be an answer and we were going to find it. We knew it was our divine, inalienable right to fulfill our destinies as The Biscuit Kings. We would not be denied.

Each and every night from that point on we would come home from our jobs and begin anew. We would refresh our attitudes, grab the mixing bowl and start over. A little more cornmeal, a bit less water. Slowly the end result began to improve. We used Sarah's tail wag as a success barometer. After a couple weeks of frustrating experimentation, our biscuits began to take on the texture, smell and golden brown finish we had been looking for. In fact, they were looking and tasting perfect . . . even better than perfect. **We were there! We had developed a great-tasting, great-looking dog biscuit!** The dogs were milling about excitedly as we baked and would snap the biscuits out of our hands, nearly taking off a finger or two with each sample.

Luckily we live in a neighborhood heavily populated with dogs. Thanks to the many great dogs who live around us, the word was barked from

hey Barney . . . Smell that

house to house . . . something special was in the oven in the house down the street, where those three big chicks lived. We began to notice a pattern: dogs and dogowners alike began to make detours in their normal walks to slowly meander by, hoping for a sample of our latest batch.

We interpreted this as an extremely pawsitive sign and encouraged further response by offering sample bags to go. We had seen our biscuits trans-

Pass-It-On PB Wafers

4 cups wholewheat flour
1/2 cup cornmeal
1 medium egg

1 cup peanuts
1 1/4 cups peanuts, chopped
1 teaspoon vanilla

1 1/4 cups water

Preheat oven to 375 degrees. Combine all ingredients. Knead by hand until thoroughly mixed. Roll into 3/4 inch patty. Cut out wafers with small round cutter (2 1/2 inch) or form small balls and flatten by hand. Bake for 50 minutes or until brown on a baking sheet sprayed with a non-stick cooking spray. Cool on a rack. Store in a sealed container. For an extra treat, dip cookies in skim milk and feed. Yield: 24 wafers.

form from burnt and hideous to glamorous and tasty and we were eager for feedback. Our neighbors began to tell us that they had never seen their dogs react so strongly to any dog biscuit. One told us of how their pup had scratched through a cabinet to get to our treats. Another admitted to coming home to find only the shreds of our sample bag left, with all the biscuits gone. It was extremely gratifying to hear those stories and our little chests swelled with pride.

Chapter 3

Mark Gets Bit

It was about this time that Mark happened upon an ad in our local paper for an upcoming dog event. It was to be sponsored by the Johnson County Mental Health Society (which probably should have told us something), and it was going to focus on the role that animals, particularly dogs, play in maintaining our mental health. Tables would be available to set up on for a fifty-dollar donation. The event was to be held in exactly two weeks. We excitedly decided that this would be a great opportunity to present ourselves for the first time to the public. Mark called and reserved a table immediately.

Our goal was to bake enough biscuits to make $1,000. We had no idea of what to expect at the show, but we wanted to be prepared. After making a list, we scraped together enough cash to go buy the necessary ingredients, some bags, a tablecloth, a sign for our display and three hundred flyers. The show was thirteen days away and we had a lot of baking to do.

Each and every day for the next two weeks we baked. We would come right home from work, head straight into the kitchen and get busy. We'd bake until midnight and then start over again at 5:00 P.M. the next day. Then for sixteen hours on Saturday and sixteen hours on Sunday. We baked frantically. And as soon as the biscuits were out of the oven, we were bagging them up and storing them in boxes. As the show approached we were getting really excited. But it started to become obvious that we were not going to be able to produce enough biscuits to earn our $1,000 goal. It was frustrating, because our little oven cooked so slowly. All we could do was the best that we could. It looked as if we were going to be able to produce somewhere around three hundred pounds. For two people, baking for two weeks. At two dollars a pound, which was what we were hoping to charge, that would be only $600. After you subtracted our costs for the show, if we completely sold out we would each make somewhere in the neighborhood of a dollar an hour as a reward for our labors. Something was terribly wrong with this picture. But, we rationalized, at least it would be a start.

Finally the big day arrived and we scurried about packing up for the show. My nephew and niece were recruited to help with the anticipated throngs. We got to the show early to have plenty of time to set up and get organized. Just before the show was scheduled to begin, we walked around to scope out our competition. We noticed a bit apprehensively that all the tables were manned by the local distributors for some very, very large companies. All the biggest names in the pet food industry were represented, each set up with an expensive display area. Humbly, with our tails tucked between our legs, we scurried back to our trashy, cheap little rented table.

Suddenly the hour arrived and we were on! We watched the first few attendees trickle in. We made sure our shirts were tucked in and checked to make sure we had nothing stuck between our teeth. Our table looked great . . . clean and simple. By the time the people began arriving at our area, we were ready with our sales pitch. Politely one person after the next would listen, smile and slowly move on. What were we doing wrong? We were asking only two dollars a pound for handcut, **100 percent all-natural, beautiful bones.** Our hearts were baked into each and every biscuit! What more could a customer want?

Finally my ten-year-old niece ran up and breathlessly announced that out of all the tables that were set up, we were the only one charging for our products. Everyone else was doling out their stuff for free! No wonder we saw people wandering past, loaded down with bag after bag of goodies. Well now, this was embarrassing. Not to mention incredibly disheartening after spending the last two weeks baking ourselves into a state of complete mental and physical exhaustion. It was with a sad and heavy heart that we removed our little homemade sign and began to hawk our treats as free. We'd show the big guys! We would just give away our one-pound bags, too. And to think that we were sad about only making a dollar an hour! **Now it was more like a negative dollar an hour!**

Short on Bread Shortbread

1/2 cup honey
1/4 cup vegetable shortening

2 teaspoons vanilla
2 cups white flour

Preheat over to 325 degrees. Mix honey, shortening and vanilla with flour. Roll into golf ball-size balls. Flatten slightly and place on a baking sheet. Bake approximately 25 minutes until slightly browned. Let cool on a rack or pan then store in a sealed container. They're dog-licious! Yield: 24 treats.

UT OH.

Boy, was that ever painful. Especially when some people would come up and say, "Well, I have five dogs" or some such statement and then they'd stand there with their bags open as if they were trick-or-treating for extra treats. We just smiled through our teeth and chatted endlessly, extolling the virtues of our great biscuit.

The glaring heat of that August 8th afternoon was relentless, which meant the crowds were much less than forecast. In fact, the entire turnout was dismal. In fact, the whole damn event had been a disaster, especially from our slave-labor point of view. At around 5:30 in the afternoon, we followed the other tables' leads and began dismantling our display. We were grouchy and embarrassed. For the first time since Mark found the bone cutter in his stocking, we asked ourselves if this was the right thing to be doing. We had tried so hard and had heard so many great things about our biscuits, it was hard for us to come to terms with such a lukewarm, indifferent reception.

Plus, to top it off, our neighbor was having a huge barbecue in his backyard and we knew he would see our truck still full of boxes when we got home. Double embarrassment! How could we explain returning home with such a large inventory? We thought about telling him someone had bought it all and asked us to deliver it the next day, but we felt he would see through that. We finally settled on just driving around until it was too dark for him to see. That night was truly one of the lowest points of our young company's history.

The next day, both of us avoided the subject of how the dog show had gone, but it was clearly weighing heavily on our minds. So you can imagine the joy, the great joy—**nay! the ecstatic rapture**—we felt, when we got

home that evening from work and found five messages on our recorder! Five people had called to tell us how much their dogs enjoyed their treats and then asked how they could order more! Da da da da HAPPY DAYS ARE HERE AGAIN! THE SKIES ABOVE ARE CLEAR AGAIN! SO LET'S SING A SONG OF CHEER AGAIN! HAPPY DAYS ARE HERE AGAIN!

Life **was** beautiful! People **were** good! God **did** want people to be happy! Those phone messages completely lifted our spirits. We immediately called the people back and arranged for convenient home delivery. In fact, one of the customers wanted to order *twenty pounds!* No problem! God knows we had enough back stock leftover from the show. We could deliver the biscuits that night, if he wanted. How's that for customer service?

Incidentally, that was the first and last time in Three Dog Bakery's history that we have had any real back stock available. From that moment on, we began to sell more than we could bake.

Our first delivery was quite a thrilling adventure. We could remember the guy because he had this incredibly huge, gigantic slobbery dog. He told us it was a Presa Canaria, a Spanish breed, and there were only five of them in the entire United States. The dog was well-behaved and lumbered alongside his owner like a rhinocerous. He literally weighed 225 pounds. Such a good doggie.

He lived at least a million miles away and we got detailed directions to his house. We drove out with his twenty-pound order, thrilled with fulfilling our first bone-ified order. We located his home and pulled excitedly into the driveway, screeching to a stop just molecules away from his house. I got out of the car, wrestled the box out of the backseat and carried it up to the front door of the house.

A few seconds later, our first customer stood in the door, holding a check for forty dollars in his hands. I swear I could see a halo around his head. Meanwhile, I had noticed Mark getting out of the car and approaching the garage door, which had been left open. As I stood there transfixed, totally absorbed in the beauty of that transcendent moment, I noticed Mark running rapidly back toward the car. Actually he was moving so fast his hair was blowing straight back.

I jolted back to reality, concluded the sale and lavished thanks and praise upon our first customer whose name we can no longer recall. I wondered if he had seen Mark's suspicious behavior. "Great," I thought, "he's going to think we stole something out of his garage." I clutched the check tightly in my paws and headed back to the car to find out why Mark was acting so strangely.

I had barely opened the car door when Mark hissed at me, "Dan, that dog bit me . . . let's get out of here!" The car's engine roared into life and I backed helter-skelter out of the driveway. When we got to the intersection at the end of the street, Mark raised his shirt with trembling hands and showed me his newly acquired battle scar.

It seems that Mark had seen the huge dog sauntering up to the garage door to investigate who had pulled into his driveway. So Mark did what any dog nut would do, he got out to play with the dog, thank him for loving our treats and scratch him behind the ears for persuading his owner to call us. But the sweet, lovable doggie turned into a **protective, raging, hell-beast** when he saw Mark encroaching on his territory. Thank God in heaven that he was attached to a secured lead. When he lunged at Mark, he was already almost fully extended on his lead and his teeth could barely graze the soft, flabby fold of Mark's white, blubbery belly. (Just kidding, Mark.)

Nonetheless, as we examined his near-fatal wound, we could literally see the indentation of every single tooth in that giant dog's mouth molded into Mark's stomach. Mark was as white as a ghost. It is not a comfortable feeling to have a two-hundred-pound snarling, drooling, white-fanged beast lunging at your stomach. Thankfully, the skin had just been grazed, but the area was already swelling up and discoloring. What a close call!

By the next day, Mark's stomach had turned into a panoramic vista of greens, purples and yellows. The following day, it was swollen, hard and inflamed, almost the size of a softball. By that point we were starting to get panicky. We called a doctor and he immediately summoned Mark to his office. He asked if we had notified the dog's owner and gotten a copy of his rabies vaccination. Of course, we hadn't.

In the months that we spent yakking about how we would run our business and planning what kind of products we would produce, we had talked at great length about the importance of providing extraordinary customer service. I truly believe that at that moment, in that doctor's office, we proved to ourselves to what astonishing levels we would take this notion. After a brief discussion of our situation, we decided it would be better for Mark to die from his dog bite than to offend our first customer by asking for a rabies certificate. What if the guy didn't reorder?

Fortunately, the swelling in Mark's stomach began to subside, followed shortly thereafter by the return of his normal coloring. All in all, not a bad ending to our first delivery.

After the initial thrill of those first reorders and Mark's near brush with death, we got serious about the business. People had often encouraged us to sell our treats to some of the local pet stores, but we had no idea how to go about doing it. God knows we gave enough business to them because of our own dogs. It would seem only fair if they would return the favor.

We plotted out a course of action. We would take a bag of biscuits out to show our vet and also to two or three of our favorite pet stores. Not having a professional sales background, we found it a bit daunting to just show up on a cold call. But much to our utter delight, we found our vet and pet stores most willing to carry our biscuits. If I remember correctly, it seems that each ordered twelve one-pound bags. Thrilling! We were so excited! We quickly returned home and began to custom bake for our first, shiny-new wholesale accounts.

It quickly became obvious to us that we were going to have to consider moving our baking operation out of our kitchen. We certainly did not have the cash flow sufficient for renting a baking commissary. We still had no equipment other than our own kitchen utensils. But in order to go out and really find accounts, especially big accounts, we were going to have to address this in a quick sort of way.

We began to set aside the money we took in from our sales. We made a wish list of equipment, at the top of which were a big mixer and a big oven. As our new wholesale accounts began to reorder, we were delirious with happiness. More reorders meant money for our equipment fund.

We began to become insatiable in our pursuit of new wholesale accounts.

One by one by one we slowly added to our list. A total of five accounts, then ten, then twenty. We were always careful to not over-promise and under-deliver. We added other wholesale accounts only when we could schedule in the baking time to supply them properly. By staggering our new orders and reorders, we found that we could bake efficiently and in sufficient quantities—for now.

Meanwhile, we began to start shopping around for the mixer and the oven of our biscuit-baking dreams. We were starting to accumulate a small bit of money, just enough to start looking in earnest for our equipment. We called used-equipment dealers and attended auctions on those rare occasions when we were not baking. Finally we found a big, upright, used mixer that could be had for the right price. Then, through a friend of a friend of a friend, we heard a rumor of a pizza parlor that was out of business, but had a huge, old-fashioned, double-stack pizza oven for sale. It was so big and we could immediately see what it would do to our baking output. We bought it on the spot.

Sarah, Dottie and Gracie were all grins, tails and whiskers when we told them of our new used equipment. We warned them that they would have to take care of it, keep it clean and appreciate it. They snorted their approval and seemed to be as excited about it as we were.

The next step was to figure out how to get the equipment to where it was going. We knew that we could not afford a separate location yet and so we decided that we would have it moved into our basement. We scheduled an equipment mover to haul it over and I'm sure he thought we were crazy. Especially when we told him what the equipment would be used for. By the time his job was over, he most certainly rued the day he ever met us.

In order to get the equipment into our basement, he had to remove handles, legs, motors, doors *and* our door jamb. Plus, the gargantuan pizza oven had to be flipped sideways, requiring two extra workmen. But finally, the dirty deed was done and we were left alone to contemplate our fun new toys. It seemed so strange to see such big pieces of commercial equipment in our basement. The dogs sniffed all about, their tails wagging their approval. Now we'll get all the treats we want. Ain't life grand? they thought.

A few days later, again using our own paychecks to fund our so-called expansion, we had our equipment properly installed. I'm sure we violated every code known to the city administrator, but we would not be denied our newfound baking pleasures. We were really getting the hang of this baking thang. Friends would drop by and we would proudly herd them down to the basement to show them our setup. Everyone ooohed and aaaahed and we felt like real business tycoons.

Now we could do in one hour what had previously taken all day. It was beautiful. We could continue to find new accounts, in addition to selling to our friends, neighbors and coworkers. It seemed that everyone approved of what we were doing. Everyone really enjoyed the fact that our biscuits were chemical-free and fresh-baked, using only fresh, wholesome ingredients. Most importantly, dogs were really digging them. Especially Sarah, Dottie and Gracie. They would lounge around like the Queens of Sheba while we toiled endlessly down in our basement.

I remember one day in particular. After Dottie had gorged herself to a point of semi-consciousness, she laid down to take a nap. I was chopping fresh carrots for our latest batch and in my haste, one of the carrot medallions rolled off the edge of the table and began to roll right toward Dottie's mouth. It zigged and it zagged and finally, seconds later, arrived right at the tip of her little, pampered, spotted snout. Without so much as even raising her head off of the concrete floor, she just leisurely opened her mouth and let the carrot roll in. The logistics and timing of that will never happen again in a million years.

And ever since then, that is about as hard as any of the girls have had to work for a treat. Thank God our biscuits are low in fat or they'd be mistaken for the Three Little Pigs. They have never grown tired of our snacks and have relished their roles as Official Taste Testers. We have calculated that on a good day, between what we offer them, what they beg from customers with those heart-rending, con-artist, "Please-feed-me-because-I-am-soooooo-hungry" stares and what they are able to forage and steal for themselves, they haul in at least one hundred treats—each. Eating all the profits, with absolutely no remorse.

Meanwhile, back in our basement, the smell of garlic began to permeate not only our entire house, but the neighborhood as well. Sometimes I would see dogs stopping in front of our house, on their leashes, with their noses up in the air deeply inhaling the aromatic fragrance. Our neighbors began moving their smart little al fresco dinner parties from their decks to the relative safety of their dining rooms. However, we both love the smell of garlic and were both taught from an early age to mistrust those who didn't. So we continued on.

We had long since started purchasing our flour in large fifty-pound bags from a mill located way out in western Kansas . . . . the heart of our great nation's wheat belt. As we increased the amount of biscuits we produced, naturally we increased the amount of flour that we were using. And flour was everywhere. Airborne flour particles began landing throughout the house, making it hard to distinguish what was flour and what was actual dust.

We knew it would not be long before we seriously had to consider a change of venues—or a maid. And we couldn't afford either. We would be tarred and feathered by our neighbors and their vigilante posse of angry dinner guests or we would have to dig out more space from underneath our house to accommodate our growth.

We had decided that if the business was ever going to turn into a real, full-time gig, we were going to have to start devoting full-time energy to it. Baking in the evenings and on weekends was fine, but it really was getting exhausting. After much discussion and heated arguments on who would be the lucky (or unlucky) one to quit his job first, we came to the mutual decision that Mark would be the one.

At the time he was working for his dad's pharmaceutical research and development company, Beckloff Associates. Generously, his dad let him cut back to four days a week, then three, then two. That was a really great way for us to slowly wean ourselves off of two incomes and to help even out the stress of making that total plunge. We realize some entrepreneurs are not afforded that luxury and we have been grateful ever since.

The downside to working at home full-time was that you were working at home full-time. Day after day. Week after week. It did not take long before Mark started showing signs of going crazy. It has been said that perhaps as many as 50 percent of the early settlers in this country may have become mentally deranged. And we could understand why. The loneliness of working around their house all day . . . limited interaction with other humans . . . the wind whistling and howling through the walls . . . all this was very much what we experienced, but Mark even more so.

We had begun to look around for a real bakery location, some place cheap that we could move into if for no other reason than to just get out of the house. We were here all the time. Plus, even more importantly, we felt an overpowering need to truly legitimize our business. For some reason, we felt that we were not a "real" business as long as it was home-based. We needed to have a real business address. I sensed the end was near when I came home one day and saw a cryptic message written in the flour/dust on the dining room table: "Looking For Space. Be Back Soon."

Chapter 4

Starting to Grrrrrow

Excitement and anticipation was in the air! And so was the thick, over-whelming odor of pungent, fresh garlic. We were fresh-baking our whole-some vegetable beef bones sixteen to eighteen hours a day and our entire three-story house reeked. The smell was in all of our furniture, drapes and clothing.

One early spring evening, I ran up to a nearby convenience store for a gallon of milk and two teenaged girls in line behind me began to complain, **"What's that smell? Something smells like dog food!"** Crimson-faced, I paid for the milk and scurried out the door with my tail between my legs and my ears folded back. How dare they compare our beautiful, all-natural, handmade-with-love bakery treats to ORDINARY DOG FOOD?

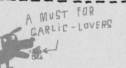
OH MY!

A MUST FOR GARLIC-LOVERS

After Din-Din Minty Mints

WHEWIE!

1/4 cup carob chips, unsweetened

1/8 teaspoon pure mint oil; suggested flavors are spearmint, wintergreen and cinnamon

12 confection candy cups

Place the cups on a tray that will fit in your refrigerator. In a small pan, on medium heat, melt carob chips. Stir in mint oil. Spoon 1/2 teaspoon of mixture into bottom of cups. Chill 10 minutes. Keep mints chilled, until gone. Oo-la-la, no more doggie breath! Yield: 12 mints

NO MORE arFUL doggie-bREath.

By April 1991, it had become obvious that we could no longer continue baking at home. This realization quickly became a souce of frustration. While we were extremely happy that our business was growing and becoming too much for a home-based operation, we were disgruntled by how much money it would take to move into any kind of real baking facility. There would be rent, security deposits, utility deposits, city licenses, additional equipment and fixtures . . . all kinds of expenses. Even though business was booming, we were nowhere near having that kind of money. We were making plenty of dough by that point . . . too bad it was all biscuit dough.

$$\neq \ \$\ ¢ \ \$$$

Our situation was a classic entrepreneur's catch-22. We would be unable to grow if we didn't move into a larger place, yet it took all of our incoming cash to finance just our ingredients and immediate, mandatory supplies. Nonetheless, we kept one eye open for any rental opportunities, miracles or combination thereof. So, lo and behold, driving home from work one day, I happened to look over and see that a small, struggling restaurant had finally folded after about a year of operation. Hmmmm, I thought, wonder how much that place rents for? I eased my truck out of the traffic flow and circled the block to inspect the premises. After jotting down the landlord's telephone number, I hopped out to peer into the darkened windows.

I could see what was the dining area and at the rear, in the shadows, the kitchen area. It was a small space, but looking back, I remember thinking it was huge compared to our basement. It was only two or three blocks from home, which was perfect. Plus, since it had already been a restaurant, it would have gas lines for our oven already installed. I started to get excited and I sped home to tell Mark of my **409 E. 33rd Street** discovery.

With visions of mass production dancing in our biscuit-baking heads, we came back later that evening and Mark agreed with my assessment. A large part of this location's beauty and appeal was that it was nestled deep in the heart of a seedy, run-down, low-rent district . . . just our kind of spot. But on the positive side, it was also situated on a very heavily traveled street that led not only to the Kansas City-based Hallmark Cards corporate office, but also continued on into the downtown area. We envisioned thousands of dog-loving workers driving past each day and gazing longingly at our sign.

When we got home, we called the landlord who turned out to be a great guy who was married to a very nice lady. And it also turned out that they lived in an apartment above the space and had lived there for some fifty-odd years. The space did come equipped with various levels of gas and electric service and also included a big industrial two-door refrigerator and a three-bay stainless steel sink. They were asking $400 a month and, yes, they would be available to show the space that very evening, if we so desired. So desired? *So desired?* We flew the three blocks and were there in two seconds.

Swept away by the sheer excitement of it all, we immediately agreed to lease the space for at least a year. Well, we agreed *after* we begged and pleaded with them to take $300 a month instead of $400. They were so nice to agree to our little Chihuahua of an offer. They probably couldn't believe the space was going to be rented that fast—or to a dog biscuit company. This area was not known as a hotbed of commercial activity by *any* stretch of the imagination.

Our first lease! This was a big, bold move on our part. By that point, we probably had about thirty little wholesale accounts comprised of veterinarian clinics and mom-and-pop pet stores. But I guarantee we didn't have enough business that we didn't feel some discomfort knowing that we were going to have to fork over three hundred bones each and every month. We now had even more inspiration to go out and sell! sell! sell! We had overhead, man.

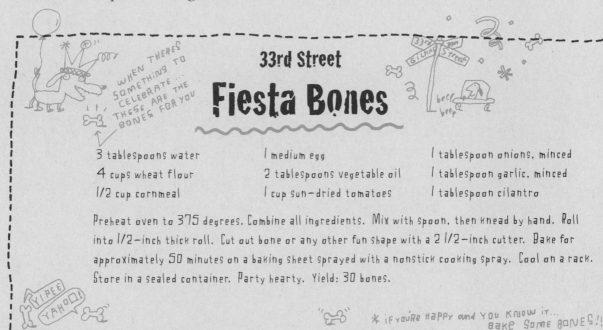

WHEN THERE'S SOMETHING TO CELEBRATE... THESE ARE THE BONES FOR YOU

33rd Street
Fiesta Bones

3 tablespoons water
4 cups wheat flour
1/2 cup cornmeal

1 medium egg
2 tablespoons vegetable oil
1 cup sun-dried tomatoes

1 tablespoon onions, minced
1 tablespoon garlic, minced
1 tablespoon cilantro

Preheat oven to 375 degrees. Combine all ingredients. Mix with spoon, then knead by hand. Roll into 1/2-inch thick roll. Cut out bone or any other fun shape with a 2 1/2-inch cutter. Bake for approximately 50 minutes on a baking sheet sprayed with a nonstick cooking spray. Cool on a rack. Store in a sealed container. Party hearty. Yield: 30 bones.

YIPEE YAHOO!

* IF YOU'RE HAPPY and YOU KNOW IT... BAKE SOME BONES!!

On the first of May 1991, just like the Beverly Hillbillies, we loaded up the truck with the sum total of our business assets and moved in. We painted the walls, scrubbed the floors and had our first sign made to hang on the outside of the building. Our excitement and enthusiasm was completely unleashed. Even Sarah's, Dottie's and Gracie's tails spun into full throttle when they were first brought into our new space. It's as if we *all* knew that it was starting to happen for us.

Sarah and Dottie immediately set out looking for mice and exploring the various cracks and crevices in the old building, while gigantic, 140-pound Gracie made sure she stayed underfoot at all times, God love her. Eventually, within days, we had the oven hooked up and all of our equipment was in place and we were ready to begin production. We were off and running.

By this time, we had begun to experiment with making other flavors of biscuits. We felt that we had the formula down perfectly for our vegetable beef treats and it was time to expand our horizons. We tried to think of all the different foods that our dogs loved. There were so many foods they savored and enjoyed: peanut butter, bananas, squirrels. When you got down to it, our dogs had robust, epicurean appetites. Since we felt there were better, easier and more fulfilling marketing opportunities to be had with peanuts than with squirrels, we decided peanut butter would be our next biscuit flavor. Again, we set out altering and experimenting with our ingredients, but this time we had months of baking experience under our collars. Our second flavor was decidedly easier to develop than our first.

After we achieved the golden brown, crunchy results we were looking for, we once again began the task of testing our newest product. We called upon neighborhood dogs, friends' dogs and coworkers' dogs to be our own personal KC-K9 guinea pigs. Our three biscuit-loving girls had immediately given the new peanut butter treats their **Two Paws Up Maximum Approval Rating** so we had a bit more confidence when we distributed the new test treats.

And once again, the response was immediate and overwhelming. Intensely positive feedback began filtering back to us. Another hit! It was so gratifying to hear those reports. Just as a sidenote, even after all these years, we get just as happy and gratified today when we listen to our customers' comments about our treats as we did back then. It's really great and one of our favorite parts of the job.

After the success of the first two treats, we became maniacs. Not only did adding a second flavor increase our wholesale sales, we were also unwittingly setting the foundation for our Bakery For Dogs. We began to develop more biscuits. It became a game almost. Soon we had six different flavors of treats in our Rover's repertoire: Vegetable Beef, Peanut Butter, Honey Granola, Toasted Coconut Almond, Oatmeal Raisin and Carob Chip.

Up until this time, we were using our new production facility for whole-sale baking only. But then we began to think, "Hey, we're here baking every day anyway, why don't we open the blinds, put out an OPEN sign and sell fresh-baked biscuits hot outta the oven?" It was really an exciting moment for us when we decided to let people come in to our bakery. It seemed like such a great idea. How could people *not* stop to buy such fresh, all-natural dog treats? Of course, we envisioned a line going out the door and halfway down the street.

After all, we were starting to get a bit of name recognition around town. From time to time, we would run into somebody who would say they had seen our products at such and such a place. Or we'd meet someone who'd say, "Oh yeah! You're the dog biscuit guys." We were starting to feel really proud of our growing little business.

Sadly, however, there were two problems that prevented our 33rd Street location from becoming a busy retail bakery. First, although we were located on a well-trafficked street, drivers were hesitant about turning off and losing their place in the traffic flow. Plus the rush of commuters was very 8:00-to-5:00 oriented; people were concerned only with getting to work and then getting home from work.

The second major strike against our location was the neighborhood itself. We didn't feel that it was that bad actually, but the perception was that it was totally crime-ridden. All day long we'd hear sirens, gunshots and the whirring of police helicopters. Yes, as the song says, everything truly *is* up-to-date in Kansas City. Suburban motorists who were passing through considered our location a war zone. But in all fairness, we were broken into only once in an entire year and a half. I'm sure the burglar was none too

the Bakery Bandits
Banana Mutt Cookies

3 cups bananas, mashed
1 teaspoon vanilla

6 cups oats
1 cup peanuts, chopped
1/3 cup applesauce, unsweetened

Preheat oven to 350 degrees.
Mix all ingredients together thoroughly. Use teaspoon to drop on baking sheet sprayed with a nonstick cooking spray and press flat. Bake for approximately 15 minutes or until slightly brown. Cool on a rack and store in an airtight container. Yield: approximately 2 dozen cookies.

PANSY.
10121 Caught Red-handed Pilfering and Plundering Banana mutt cookies.

Lulu the Looter Loves + Pasta!

happy when all he saw was barrels full of dog biscuits. He did get our radio, though, so for a while we had no tunes while we baked. **Too bad we didn't have a three-hundred-pound snarling rottweiler to chew the legs off our nocturnal visitor.** That would have been great.

Ever so slowly, cautious, curious shoppers would drift in, sometimes just to see what in the heck was going on in the space. But we began to notice that once a customer came in, he or she always came back for more. That was a really good feeling. We made a little cardboard box with dividers in it to store our money in. Fortunately, no one came in with a fifty- or a hundred-dollar bill as we certainly would not have been able to make change. I don't think we ever kept more than twenty dollars in our homemade cash register.

To be quite honest, a busy retail day usually translated to about five customers. Thank God, we were mainly wholesaling. An absolute madhouse day was ten to fifteen customers. Looking back, it was just as well. Slow retail days gave us the time we needed to begin to fully develop our concept.

My brother Tim, who is a carpenter, mentioned to me that he had been doing a remodeling job at a local supermarket and they were getting ready to throw out a perfectly good bakery case. It was old and used and needed to be cleaned up, but if we were interested he would deliver it to us instead of the dump. Heck yes, we wanted it! We were very thrilled to have it and after we cleaned it up we discovered it even had lights in it. This was great!

Our little bakery was so silly. We would take our baking trays fresh out of the oven and place them into our new/used bakery case. It held six trays perfectly . . . one tray for each flavor. Now, when customers came in, they could peruse our selection of baked bones and make their decisions. "Hmmm . . . let's see . . . I'll have five peanut butter biscuits, two honey granola and throw in a dozen vegetable beef," they'd say. And we, in all earnestness, would take our tongs and carefully place their treats into a doggie bag. People frequently commented on how good things smelled and what an interesting and novel idea we had going. Again, it was all those little bits of praise and positive reinforcement that kept us salivating like the proverbial **Pavlovian dogs.**

Pavlov's Punkin' Bread

1 medium egg	1/2 teaspoon cinnamon	1 cup pumpkin, cooked
1 2/3 cups whole wheat flour	1/4 teaspoon nutmeg	1/2 cup water
1 teaspoon baking soda	1/2 cup applesauce	1 4 x 8" bread pan sprayed with
1 teaspoon baking powder	1/2 cup honey	nonstick cooking spray

Preheat oven to 350 degrees. Combine dry ingredients. In separate medium-size mixing bowl, combine wet ingredients. Gradually add dry mixture to wet, mixing thoroughly. Pour into bread pan. Bake for 50 minutes, or until a toothpick inserted in center comes out dry. Cool the bread on a rack. Store in a sealed container. Yield: 1 loaf of bread.

*it doesn't take a bell...just a sniff or a smell!

One of the really nice things about our 33rd Street customers was that most of them were truly interesting people. Even though the area sucked, 90 percent of our customers were very successful business owners, local personalities and executive-type people. Occasionally we would get a flock of suburban housewives making a mad dash for our front door from the sanctuary of their BMWs and Mercedes Benzes. One would usually say, "I've been meaning to stop in for some time now, but I wanted to wait until my girlfriends were with me." I'm here to say that the neighborhood *really isn't that bad*. But, as they say, perception is everything.

We made a point of learning every one of our customers' (and their dogs') names. We wanted everyone to know just how important their business was to us. And it was no exaggeration . . . we did **greatly** appreciate their patronage. Our customers were helping us pay the gas bill, plus we were making new friends as well. I think everyone who walked in the door knew how hard we were trying and I hope that feeling is still obvious to our new customers today. The gratitude we feel toward our customers and our commitment to providing extraordinary customer service is every bit as strong today as it was back then.

One of our earliest marketing strategies was to become closely aligned with the area animal shelters and rescue centers. Right from the start we knew we wanted to help less fortunate dogs and to give something back to the canine community that we loved so much. We would fantasize endlessly about the day when we had so much cash flow that we could make some hefty donations to help ease the financial burdens that these organizations face daily.

It is still very much our dream to fund a Three Dog Bakery wing at one of the local shelters. **WE LOVE DOGS!** Naturally this wish makes Sarah, Dottie and Gracie very happy. Especially Sarah, since she personally knows the cold, hard, lonely terror of incarceration. We are proud to report that we have contributed each and every year to area shelters and each year our cash and product donations have grown more substantial. We urge the readers of this book to **please, please give generously to your community's animal shelters.** It is so rewarding and it will make you feel so good. Even if you can't give money, give time! Give newspapers! Give paper towels! Drop off some dog food! Anything helps, no matter how small.

The saddest thing is that spaying and neutering dogs has become so safe, easy and cheap and yet many people still don't or won't do it. **Pet overpopulation could be such an easy problem to solve if everyone would just do their part.** It is a national disgrace that our educated, affluent country must destroy so many millions and millions of beautiful, lovable, funny dogs and cats year after year after year. And it is literally millions—each year! So sad and so very unnecessary. Mahatma Gandhi once said the measure of a nation's true greatness lies in the way its citizens treat their animals. The answer is education and while the situation is improving, I know and you know we can do better.

But let me step off of the doghouse and get back to the bakery. We wanted more proprietary products and we would not be denied! Soon we added "Pound" cakes™, Pupcakes®, CiaoWow Cheese Pizzas®, Kansas City style barbecue Slab O' rrrRRRibs® and CollieFlowers® to our menu. We discovered the pure, unadulterated joys of carob, fresh fruits and vegetables and their place in our product mix. We began to learn more and more about the actual science of dough mixing and baking. Granted, we were learning most of it through the school of hard knocks but we were actually getting better and better at it. Each week our mound of burnt treats became smaller.

Soon we had carrot, banana and carob chip birthday cakes. Then Boxer Brownies®. We learned how to decorate, frost and pipe icing. I'm sure our first pathetic cakes sold more out of pity than artistic merit. **But God Bless Dogs! Never critical! Always appreciative!** They enjoyed the great KC-K9 flavor of their personalized cakes even if it wasn't the most beautiful presentation. Our customers began bringing in photos of their dogs eating their cakes on their birthdays and we would post them on our wall. Dogs themselves began showing up to pick up their treats—sometimes without their owners. And we were loving every minute of it.

Not only were we going to town on new product development, we were also finding new wholesale accounts. We would set goals for ourselves, then cruelly laugh and point at each other when we fell short. Soon we had forty, then fifty, then sixty wholesale accounts. Sometimes the accounts would develop into high-turnover, steady reorderers and other times we were clearly barking up the wrong tree. We were constantly learning.

I was still working at my job and I was very jealous that Mark was able to devote himself wholly to KC-K9. I desperately longed to quit my job, too! But it was just impossible. Even with all our increased business, after the bills were paid there was really no money left. It was incredibly frustrating. I was going to KC-K9 after my day job and working all weekend, too. We were both in a per-*pet*-ual state of exhaustion.

Plus, I was spending more and more of my time at Western Auto, my daytime job, on the phone secretly conducting KC-K9 business. Each week

20 Steel BELTED RADIALS 595
*6 PUPCAKES
40 TIRE IRONS #792B
   10 dipped bones
10 JUMPER CABLES LOT 7
*2 bags box of brownies
*1 box of RRRIBS
*COLLIE FLOWERS 6 basss

we would call every wholesale account we had to see how our biscuits were selling and to ask if they needed more. At first Mark was able to make the calls, but as our client list grew, we simply could not afford to give up precious baking time to make those important calls. So, every Thursday at 9:00 A.M. I would begin calling accounts from my cubicle at work. In a barely audible voice I would whisper, "Hello, this is Dan Dye, calling from KC-K9 Bakery and I was wondering how your biscuit supply is holding out." Then I would proceed to conduct business, taking and repeating orders, tallying up totals and checking dates for deliveries. Usually the entire transaction would be completed in a low, husky voice. I often wondered if the person on the other end of the line thought I was a per-

(Macintosh) Apple Crunch PupCakes®

2 3/4 cups water
1/4 cup applesauce, unsweetened
1/8 teaspoon vanilla
4 cups whole wheat flour

1 cup dried apple chips
1 tablespoon baking powder
1 medium egg
2 tablespoons honey powder

Muffin pans (total capacity 12–14), sprayed with a nonstick cooking spray

Preheat oven to 350 degrees. Mix wet ingredients thoroughly. Combine dry ingredients in separate bowl, mix thoroughly. Add wet ingredients to dry and mix well, scraping sides and bottom to be sure no dry mixture is left. Pour into muffin pans. Bake for 1 1/4 hour or until a toothpick inserted in center comes out dry. Store in a sealed container. Yield: 12–14 pupcakes.

vert. I was also using the computer equipment in my cube to design our bags' labels, store signage and letterhead. Thank God I had access to that equipment! I don't know what we would have done without it. I justified my use of the equipment by saying it was helping me learn the Macintosh better, thereby making me a better employee. (Hahaha.) I have often wondered when it will all catch up with me, and I am trying to work off my karmic debt to Western Auto—in fact, one more steel-belted radial purchase and I think I'll be paid in full.

Life rolled along and soon we had close to one hundred wholesale accounts. It was too beautiful for words. Little would anyone have guessed that we were still, yes still, cutting the biscuits out by hand one by one by one. In fact, in August 1991, Mark calculated that he had cut out over two hundred thousand biscuits by hand! He actually had a biscuit shape callused into his hand. It was completely out of control. I was coming home tired from working all day, then having to start all over again at 5:00 P.M.

There was no way we could afford some big machine to make our lives easier. We knew we certainly didn't have the collateral for a bank loan. So we started really sniffing around to find someone who could make us a faster bone cutter. We finally found a toolsmith who was able to fashion a handheld cutter that would cut eight biscuits out at once! Although he charged what we felt to be an exorbitant sum, we were able to pay him and guess what? We instantly became eight times faster! Our output each day became eight times greater! Better living through modern technology!

It wasn't long after that when we splurged again and had a special machine made for us by a couple of guys who were starting their business, too. Our new machine would cut out **thirty-two biscuits at a time**, but we still hand-kneaded every ounce of dough that we produced. We felt that we had taken a quantum leap in our production capacity. We were really ready for the big time now. We also took out our first bank loan for $5,000, using our cars as collateral, to pay for our new, desperately needed toy.

In the meantime, we were getting a wee taste of the retail bug . . . and we liked it. We really enjoyed meeting the people who were buying our products and the dogs who were eating them. We wondered how many dogs lived in Kansas City and pondered how we could convince them (or their owners) to come into our bakery. We still couldn't afford to advertise in any of the local papers, so we began to set up at flea markets and sidewalk fairs. We loved it when someone would come up and tell us that they bought our treats at their pet store.

We tried anything and everything to get our name out there, within our extremely limited budget. We printed up flyers with coupons and tied them on our neighbors' front doors. We kept samples in our cars and passed them out to people we passed who were walking their dogs. We tacked our business cards onto community bulletin boards. Then one beautiful, sunny Sunday in April 1992, we had an exciting experience that was to forever alter the course of our little company.

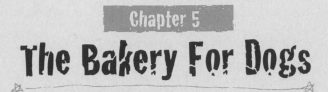

Chapter 5

The Bakery For Dogs

Those of you who know Mark and me will acknowledge that we both speak often about the Guardian Angel who watches over our company. Throughout the years we have actually experienced and witnessed many miracles in our lives. And for you cynics out there, as we once were, if they *weren't* actual miracles, they were at least some pretty strange coincidences.

There are a million and one reasons why we could—and should—have gone out of business at any given time . . . lack of funds, lack of business know-how, lack of planning, you name it. Even huge, established, well-funded companies can fall prey to those traps. But it sure seems as though every time we were reaching a rock-bottom low, if we continued to work hard and think positively, miracles happened. Some may call it luck, we call it divine intervention. There's an old adage: The harder you work, the luckier you get. And while we totally believe in that, sometimes good fortune involves more than just hard work.

Sometimes miracles were very small things; checks that would arrive in the mail on the day we absolutely, positively needed them in the worst possible way. Or perhaps it would come in the form of an ingredient supplier who offered us great payment terms when he really had no reason to do so. Or deciding to use a certain, obscure store fixture and then going out and stumbling upon it immediately—at a dirt cheap, close-out price. All kinds of small miracles began to unfold around us and sometimes we weren't even aware they were taking place. Miracles happen every day to everyone . . . all we have to do is open up to them, be aware of them, be thankful for them.

And so it happened that one beautiful, sunny Sunday in April 1992, we had an opportunity to knock off work at noon. We had found ourselves completely caught up on our wholesale orders and our little retail shop was closed on Sundays. An afternoon off! This was unheard of! We had spent the previous two years working and baking every blessed day. And when I say "every day," I mean Christmas, Thanksgiving and every other holiday as well. We *literally* had not taken a day off in over two years, so you can imagine how much fun it was to be able to go do something—*anything*—on this unexpectedly free afternoon.

It was such a beautiful day that we decided to just jump in the car and drive somewhere. We hopped on the interstate and began heading north out of Kansas City, with no idea where we were heading. We rolled down the windows, cranked up the radio and sped away, delirious with the sweet feeling of complete freedom. After we had traveled a few miles, we decided that our journey would be to a little town forty-five miles north of Kansas City called Weston.

Weston, Missouri, is a really cool little town. Located on the winding Missouri River, it was established around 1837. At one point it was the last trading post that the settlers could stop at before venturing on into the vast and unknown territories of the great West. Then, in 1855, a great flood occurred and by the time the river receded, the little town of Weston was left high and dry—the mighty Missouri had rerouted itself over two miles away.

This, of course, spelled the end for Weston. No longer accessible by river-boat, its usefulness as a port of commerce and trading was over. But, the river's new course was a great stroke of luck for the little settlement of Possum Trot, farther downstream. Now that Weston was no longer competition, Possum Trot went on to become known as Kansas City.

The city of Weston is located in the rolling hills of northwestern Missouri. For those of you unfamiliar with this part of the country, it is enormously beautiful land. Off of the **twisting, turning** country highways are rustic, hundred-year-old family farms, set against peaceful, pastoral backgrounds. After a thirty-minute cruise through all the ruralness, I swear you'll be ready to buy a cow and a pitchfork.

ROCKY ROADTRIP CAROB BARS

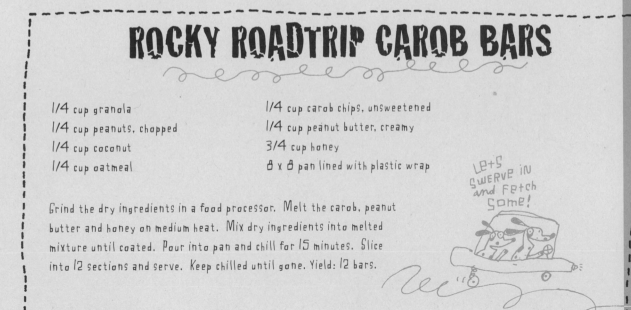

1/4 cup granola
1/4 cup peanuts, chopped
1/4 cup coconut
1/4 cup oatmeal

1/4 cup carob chips, unsweetened
1/4 cup peanut butter, creamy
3/4 cup honey
8 x 8 pan lined with plastic wrap

Grind the dry ingredients in a food processor. Melt the carob, peanut butter and honey on medium heat. Mix dry ingredients into melted mixture until coated. Pour into pan and chill for 15 minutes. Slice into 12 sections and serve. Keep chilled until gone. Yield: 12 bars.

LET'S SWERVE IN and FETCH SOME!

What is great about Weston is that the entire town looks the same today as it did 150 years ago. All of the storefronts and facades along Main Street are still intact. There are dozens and dozens of perfectly preserved antebellum homes surrounding the "downtown" area. You feel as if you are walking around some old ghost town from the Wild West. Today, however, the shops are bed and breakfasts, wineries, antique shops, art galleries and restaurants.

We were excited as we pulled into the main shopping district. We parked the car and scrambled out, eager to begin our fun-filled day of leisure. The first thing that Mark said once we arrived was, "Wow! Look at all the people here!" It was true. The sidewalks were packed with shoppers and strolling tourists. We even saw a few dogs on leashes. Immediately we looked at each other and knew what the other was thinking.

We visited a few of the stores, getting more excited as we witnessed the cash transactions going down inside. After a couple of hours, we stopped into the Weston Bakery, located at 408 Main Street, for a treat. We hadn't brought much money with us, so all we could afford were some cookies for our lunch. As we sat and gobbled down our snack, we contemplated how a little space like the Weston Bakery would be perfect for *our* bakery. We discussed, for the millionth time, how nice it would be to have a location where there were actually people around. (Here's an important FREE business tip: always remember to locate your retail business where shoppers can be found.) And finally, how much rent could a place like Weston possibly charge, for crying out loud?

We left the bakery, each lost in his own thoughts. As we strolled past the storefronts, we suddenly found ourselves in front of the Weston Development office, which was staffed by a friendly lady who was there to help people find what they were looking for. We stopped in on a whim and very cautiously began asking a few business-related questions. She caught on quickly and asked us if we were interested in finding a retail space in Weston. We were reluctant to answer since, again, we had no real cash flow for deposits, build outs, etc. In fact, it felt as if we were in the same situation as when we first moved the business out of our house.

It always felt a little, uh, strange trying to describe our unique concept to people, especially since we were still defining and refining it. When we revealed that we were looking for a bakery space (we left out the part about dogs), her face took on a strange, puzzled look. "That's odd," she murmured. "I just hung up, not five minutes ago, with the landlords of the Weston Bakery. Their tenant is moving out the first of the month and they told me to keep my eyes and ears open." Talk about your miracles!

While she didn't know how much the space rented for, she gladly gave us the landlord's telephone number. Needless to say, the entire trip home was filled with talk of moving our bakery to Weston. We were so excited. Yes, it would be a long way to drive every day, but look at all the tourists shopping there! We were incredibly curious about how much rent they would charge for the little space.

When we got home, we dashed in to call the landlord; a really nice guy who agreed to meet us at the bakery later on in the week. The good news— the GREAT news—was that the rent was no more than we were currently paying! We felt unbelievably lucky. Our timing could not have been more perfect. Jeez, our first day off in two years and we literally stumble upon a great new space at the same rent! We *did* have a Guardian Angel!

There were some really nice aspects to the space. Because of its forty-five-minutes-from-Kansas City location, it certainly would not conflict or compete with any of our whole-sale accounts. And, with all the tourists traveling through Weston, we would be able to introduce our great treats to a lot of people who wouldn't have otherwise been aware of them. It was going to be great! There was a flip side of the dog tag, however. Was this charming, laid-back country community ready for **The World's First Bakery For Dogs?** Were *we* ready for them? We pondered the "redneck factor" . . . would a group of toothless, demented farmhands show up one day and hogtie us for "tryin' to start one of them there fancy big city idees here in ar' town"? And all of these thoughts were in addition to that dreaded forty-five-minute drive each way.

When we finally were able to meet the landlords, Kent and Kathy Drew, and see the space, most of our fears were put to rest. (Except the farmhand uprising.) Then, unbelievably, we were told that the lease price also included all of the bakery equipment. Let me repeat that: THE RENT PRICE INCLUDED THE USE OF ALL THEIR BAKERY EQUIPMENT! Let me dry the tear from my eye. It was all too, too beautiful. We decided then and there to sign the lease.

CITY MERCHANT'S LICENSE

STATE OF MISSOURI
COUNTY OF PLATTE } Know All Men By These Presents
CITY OF WESTON

That ......KCK9, Inc......

having paid the City Collector of the City of Weston, Platte County, Missouri, the sum of $10.00 ......in conformity with City Ordinances, is hereby licensed to carry on the business of ...baking pet treats... at ......408 Main Street......in the City of Weston for a term ending ......December 31, 1992......

WITNESS our hands this the ...25th... day of ...Aug......, 19..92..

Barbara Lukow
Mayor.

Mary Hayworth
Clerk.

Kathleen Carter
Collector.

№ 1925

Daniel A. Dye

We hated to tell our current landlords that we were moving out. They had been so nice to us and had never so much as made a comment to us about the garlic smell that I'm sure wafted endlessly into their upstairs apartment. Plus, we had the guilty feeling that our rent payments were a very important supplement to their monthly social security checks. But there was just no other choice. We had to say, "To hell with them, let them starve! We're on our way!" No, we truly did feel terrible about leaving, but we had fulfilled our year obligation and we had been good tenants. They understood completely, wished us all the best, and told us not to forget them when we made it. Just in case you're wondering, they turned right around and rented their space after we left; we felt good about that.

We spent the next couple of weeks driving up to Weston when we could, just to look at our new space. We couldn't wait for the bakery to move out so we could move in. When we finally did get the key, we were able to take measurements and make sure that all of our stuff would fit. Once again we lucked out in that we didn't have to run gas lines, electricity or anything. It was already set up to be a bakery. We loved saving money, especially on things like that. We still do.

We didn't actually do much to the space other than move our equipment and accessories in. We hired a sign painter to paint our logo on the big plate glass window in front. He was unable to get to our job though, until the day we were scheduled to open. Although we didn't like that, we had no other choice; he was the cheapest painter we could find.

We will never forget our nervousness and excitement on that day. We felt like we were taking a quantum leap in our business. We met the painter there early the Saturday morning of our Grand Opening, and we busied our-selves with the final, finishing touches for our opening while he worked very silently and very, very quickly. By 9:00 A.M., he had the entire KC-K9 logo done and it looked great. He then started to paint on our selling tag line, **THE BAKERY FOR DOGS**, underneath the logo. By then, the shoppers and tourists were starting to show up to begin their day of shopping and fun. Slowly, a small crowd began to gather in front of our shop, curious what KC-K9 meant. It was almost time for us to open. We peered into the faces of the crowd as the painter completed his assignment. We could read their lips as they mouthed the words, "The Bakery For Dogs"?

Finally 10:00 arrived. The shelves were stocked, the bakery case was loaded with PupCakes® and PupTarts® and CollieFlowers®. The floors were sparkling and clean. Sarah, Dottie and Gracie were milling about impatient-ly, like a small herd of wildebeest, waiting to greet their first customers. Mark walked over to unlock the door and I adjusted my apron. Customers began filing in immediately.

"A bakery for dogs?" one gentleman asked incredulously.

"Is this for real?" queried another.

"Ooh. . .I just love this!" I heard a lady squeal in a shrill voice.

"Honey, come see the Scottie Biscotti®! And the SNICKERPOODLES®! What do you think Max would want?"

"Everything," her husband replied.

64

In mere moments our little bakery was filled with shoppers. At one point, Mark gestured with his head for me to look over at our oak barrels, which were filled with fresh-baked biscuits. There were customers standing in front of each barrel, all filling their sacks. It was a beautiful, beautiful sight and something neither of us will ever forget.

We couldn't believe it. Our dream was coming true. After a year of never really having any customers, in less than fifteen minutes after opening our door, we had a shop full of people and had already rung up five sales. Mark was busy retrieving pastries from the bakery case and I stood behind the register with a dazed half-smile on my face. Every now and then, throughout the day, Mark and I would just look at each other and burst out laughing. We were so incredibly happy.

All day long we listened to our customers say, "What a fabulous idea!" and "This is great! I can't wait to bring my dog here!" We were thrilled beyond description. We were talking nonstop to each and every customer about how good our ingredients were and how fresh. We invited our customers back and begged them to bring their dogs.

The day flew by and when we locked the door that night, it was almost 10:00. It occurred to us at that point that we hadn't even taken a break for lunch. Our eyes were glazed over and our voices were hoarse. Even Sarah, Gracie and Dottie were crashed out on the floor. It also struck us that our stock was dangerously low and the shelves were looking dismally barren. The next day was a Sunday and we were scheduled to be open from noon to 5:00. We had no other choice . . . we had to start baking for the next day or we wouldn't make it.

Even though we were dead tired, we were still flying high. We had made more money that day than we were used to making in two months at our 33rd Street location. Things were really changing for us, we felt. We had made the right decision.

So we took a quick inventory of what we absolutely had to bake for the next day, rolled up our sleeves and got busy baking. By the time we finished, it was almost 3:00 A.M. and we were totally exhausted. We contemplated sleeping in the bakery, but we would have to take a shower the next morning. Not to mention how ugly it would look if someone should walk by and look in the window and see me, Mark, Sarah, Dottie and Gracie all sprawled out on the floor, snoring. We dragged our bodies, limp and spent, into the car and drove the forty-five minutes back home, wondering what the next day would bring.

Lil' Ginger's
Late-Night Snaps

1/2 cup vegetable oil
1/2 cup honey
1 small egg

1 cup molasses
1 1/2 tablespoons dried ginger
3 cups white flour

1 teaspoon baking soda
1/2 teaspoon baking powder
2 teaspoons cinnamon

Preheat oven to 350 degrees. Mix all dry ingredients well. Add wet ingredients. Knead thoroughly by hand. Roll dough into quarter-size balls. Place on a baking sheet sprayed with a nonstick cooking spray. Flatten balls on baking sheet with fork. Bake approximately 15 minutes or until brown. Cool on a rack. Store in a sealed container. Yield: 24 cookies.

SNAP OUT OF IT, GRACIE, we got bones to BAKE!

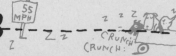

Chapter 6
Refining and Defining

Our second day of business in Weston was a repeat performance of our first. We were incredibly busy nonstop and we loved every minute of it. Even the girls were digging it. They would greet each new customer with a bark and woof and tail-waggling galore. Then they would stand or sit, looking cute as little bug's ears, while the adoring masses fawned over them, petted them, scratched them on their chests, behind the ears, on their tummies and then discreetly passed secret treats to them. Whatta life! I have often wondered, now that we've been operating our bakeries for so long, if Sarah, Dottie and Gracie think all dogs have this kind of a life.

Unfortunately, during the week there was absolutely no retail traffic in Weston, which actually turned out to be a mixed blessing. We LOVED having the extra cash flow that retail dollars brought to us, so in that sense we hated it when it was dead. But it was a blessing because the five quiet weekdays gave us an opportunity to continue baking for our wholesale accounts. In fact, it worked out perfectly this way. We could bake all week, basically uninterrupted by customers, get our deliveries done on Fridays and then have a blowout retail weekend. YEE-HAW!

We continued to define our Bakery For Dogs concept, blazing our own trail as we went. Being an original is a thrilling experience because there is no actual right or wrong way to do anything. There was no one to copy, no existing models or prototypes on which to base our operations. So we learned early on to trust our guts. If something felt right to us, we did it. If it didn't feel right, we left it alone. To this day, we operate that way and many of our biggest decisions as a corporation are made using the ol' Trust-Your-Gut rule. So far, it's never let us down.

We always remembered to let our customers know how much we valued their patronage. We're pretty sure that some of our early sales were made as much because the customers felt sorry for us as for any other reason. But Mark and I both made sure that people left knowing that their business was deeply appreciated and they had bought some darn good dog treats, too. We always stressed the fact that we add no salt, no sugar, no artificial chemicals or preservatives to any of our products; every ingredient we use is wholesome and fresh. In fact, if the human purchaser was curious, he or she could feel **GREAT** about eating our treats themselves. We would stress the fact that we donate a percentage of our profits to help neglected and abused dogs. These things are terribly important to us and we felt they would be so to our customers as well. We were right.

We also listened carefully to our customers. We have met tens of thousands of dogs and have heard tens of thousands of dog stories, and we love them. And by paying close attention to our customers, we were able to determine the kinds of products they wanted from us. We have tried to expand our horizons in many different ways at Three Dog Bakery while at the same time staying true to our founding precepts.

In the meantime, back in Weston, the days drifted lazily into weeks. We continued to find new wholesale accounts, which was always exciting to us. We had no real sense of urgency about getting our treats to market on a national level. Every now and then, a so-called business expert would come in and begin expounding on our "window of opportunity" to get our name out there. **Window Schmindow!** We were in this for dogs, not money. But to tell you the truth, deep down inside we were so proud of our products, and we knew how great they were, that we wanted them to be available everywhere.

Garden Veggie
Bagel Shmagel

1/2 cup wheat flour
2 1/2 cups white flour
1 teaspoon vegetable oil

1 medium egg
1/4 teaspoon baking powder
1/4 teaspoon baking soda

1/2 cup carrots, chopped
1/2 cup spinach, chopped
1 tablespoon garlic, minced
3/4 cup water

Preheat oven to 350 degrees. Combine dry ingredients, then add wet. Mix, then knead by hand. Form into ping-pong-ball size. Flatten, then poke hole in the center. Form into bagel shape. Bake for 50 minutes on baking sheet sprayed with nonstick cooking spray. Cool on a rack. Store in a sealed container. Serve. Yield: 16 bagels.

thud.

We also began noticing that our retail bakery sales were increasing. The word, in its most tiny form, was getting out about The Bakery For Dogs in Weston. Customers began stopping in on Tuesdays and Wednesdays, saying that they had driven in especially to come to our bakery.

We always felt so good when we'd hear that. It made us want to work even harder so we would always make their trip worthwhile. We also began to observe a lot of the locals stopping in. Weston had two separate sets of customers: its tourists and all their tourism dollars and the people who lived there. We stayed out of the town politics, but we used to hear angry stories about the clash between the ones who wanted Weston to stay as it was and those who wanted it to grow.

But we used to get the biggest kick when an overall-clad farmer would pull up in his farm truck, look both ways to make sure no one was looking, then hurry into the bakery to buy treats for his hunting dog. Once they broke the ice and came on in, they always came back, sometimes with their dogs. We never could figure out why they seemed to be embarrassed to show that they loved their dogs. I guess having the bakery there gave them "permission" to indulge their little buddies.

One thing that began to happen to us while we were in Weston which caught us completely off guard was mail order. We had not anticipated being in the mail-order business at all. Tourists passed through and they'd buy our things, bring them home and discover that their dogs loved them. Then they'd pick up the phone and call us for more, which was great. The first time a customer called and asked if we shipped, we didn't miss a beat. "Sure we do," we replied confidently.

"How do you ship?" she asked.

And literally, and we do mean literally, the UPS man was right outside our door getting a delivery together for our neighbor. "Uhhhh, we use, uhhh, UPS. Yeah, that's who we use . . . UPS." And that's how we started up in the mail-order business. Luckily for us, she didn't ask how much we charged for shipping because we would have had no idea what to say. As it was, we had to dig around for a cardboard box to ship her order in.

Over the years we have had the pleasure of meeting many successful entrepreneurs who have similar stories to tell. It seems that one of the most common traits to be found in true entrepreneurs is that they say, "Yes, we do" or "Yes, we will" and *then* they figure out how they'll get the job done. In that same vein, we can recall contacting huge potential wholesale accounts such as Bloomingdale's in New York, while we were still hand-cutting our biscuits one by one around the kitchen table! I don't know what we would have done if they had said yes.

By this point we had been in business for around two years, and we had not experienced anything but positive feelings and positive feedback from anyone with whom we came into contact. Then one day, out of the blue, we had quite the shock. Mark called me at my office (yes, I was still working at my copywriting job, but not for much longer!) and said, "Dan! Let me read you something! We're in today's *Weston Chronicle*!" At first, I was excited, since we had always welcomed any publicity and it helped people to know about us. But I could tell from the quaking in Mark's voice that something was not right. It turned out the *Weston Chronicle* had a front-page story, written tongue-in-cheek, about the horrible, overbearing garlic smell wafting out of the new bakery for dogs. They had not even contacted us for any sort of counterpoint.

We felt hurt and took it very personally. We decided that people just heard the words "dog treats" or "dog food" and immediately conjured up dirty, carcinogenic chemicals and dead cow parts. How could anyone complain if they only knew what kind of wholesome, yummy ingredients we used? Remember, it all goes back to mistrusting anyone who doesn't love garlic.

Many of the friends that we had made in Weston came to our defense after reading the story. Finally, through a weird series of events, we discovered the source of the story. Our neighbor in Weston at that time had a broken-down, crummy business that resold garage sale junk at a huge profit. We had never met her, but it turned out she became obsessively, insanely jealous of our success, while her business languished. So she began complaining to the city council about the smell.

One day, shortly after the story ran, she decided to make a scene. It was a Saturday afternoon and our shop was packed with customers. She was a very short woman and let's just call her "pleasingly plump." She elbowed her way to the front of the line and tightened her stern little face into a frowning red tomato. She began shouting about the smell and what were we going to do about it? As she screamed, the veins in her neck darkened and her multiple chins quivered with frustration and hatred. Her eyes blazed with a demonic frenzy. She was so angry she seemed to be floating six inches off the floor. We thought she was going to have a heart attack.

We were almost believing her impassioned, hell-on-wheels tirade. Even Sarah, Dottie and Gracie looked on with their ears pulled back and their heads cocked. They had never seen such a display. Neither had we. But then, she carried her rampage just a wee bit too far. She screamed, "All of my employees have been passing out from the smell and I'm going to sue you!"

At that point, the sad reality of her little tantrum really began sinking in. We had all been staring at her, speechless, not even knowing how to react. Then Diane, one of our first employees, suddenly burst out into a loud, heartfelt belly laugh. She later confessed it was the line about all her employees passing out . . . that was just carrying it too far. Then Mark joined in the laughter and so did I. Several of the customers, who had been shocked at first, began laughing too. Even Sarah, Dottie and Gracie began howling and pointing with their paws. It was just like a scene from a farce. Everyone began laughing louder and louder and she was soon reduced to a quivering, lifeless blob. But when she left our shop, she gave me one of the evilest looks I've ever seen. We've learned since then that the road to business success isn't always lined with roses. We have encountered lots of little irritants along our way.

We had been in Weston for a little over a year at that point and we were starting to get our nomadic, gypsy itch to move on again. We had spent the year constantly learning more about how to run our retail business, our mail-order business and our wholesale business. We knew the vast majority of our retail and wholesale clients were in Kansas City. Plus, the long drive each way to Weston was really growing old. We began to think in earnest about opening up a second location, back in KC.

Now that we had a halfway thriving retail business, we had a bit more cash flow. With dogged determination we began scouting out new locations.

For the first time in our company's three-year history, we were looking for a "real" location. We were excited. Until we discovered that "real" locations charge "real" rent. Wow! Spaces were expensive. Plus, we had to be very careful about where we located our second bakery, as we truly did not want to compete with any of our wholesale accounts. We really appreciated their support and did not want to tick any of them off.

After searching for quite some time and wading through all our opportunities, we finally decided on an area of Kansas City known as Westport. It was one of the oldest areas of the city, but it had enjoyed somewhat of a renaissance in the past decade. Many of the buildings had been there since the 1850s when Westport was a trading post and supply station for the covered wagons heading west on the Santa Fe trail. The ambiance of the neighborhood was bohemian, lots of art students, aging hippies and yuppies. In fact, it probably has more of an overall visitor mix than any other area of Kansas City.

The rents were high . . . much, much higher than anything we had been used to paying. This was very scary to us. We had been able to stay in business by always carefully watching our expenses and never going into debt for anything. Suddenly we were going to be faced with rent for two locations plus increased labor costs, utilities, supplies, etc. We began asking successful friends and customers for advice. Everyone seemed to think it would be a good move for us. We tried to ask people whose advice we truly valued. But no one really knew what our financial limitations were, nor did they fully understand the whole picture. We ultimately relied on our gut instincts and once again, as always, they proved to be right.

"SOUL"   GUT

Chapter 7

Thank You, Richard Gibson, Wherever You Are

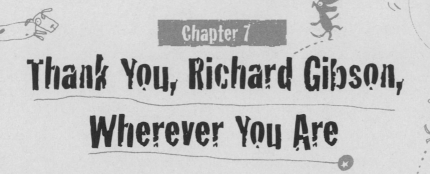

Mark and I were nervous about the big jump in rent we were facing. Our first high-profile location! But when we saw the sparkles in Sarah's, Dottie's and Gracie's eyes, we knew we had to do it. Every time I would ask Sarah, who is so wise and business-like, "Do you want to move to Westport?" she would bark and wag her tail extra hard. Then I would ask her, in the same tone of voice, "Do you even know what Westport is?" and she would bark again and wag her tail even harder.

After we had signed our lease, we couldn't wait to get opened. The more we saw our new space, the more we loved it. Westport is a very popular Kansas City tourist and entertainment district. We had fifteen hundred square feet, which was huge compared to what we were used to, right in the heart of Westport Square at 4116 Pennsylvania Avenue. There were two large display windows in front and a beautiful recessed front door. One of the most important attractions of the space was that it didn't conflict or compete with any of our wholesale accounts, which was very important to us. We would drive by the storefront at all times of day and night, wondering how well we would do there.

Although we were 99 percent thrilled with the location and the physical layout of the space, there was one huge downside. The property was a dump. It had not been taken care of or maintained in any way. It was also the first location that we had ever moved into that had not been a kitchen or bakery before. This meant we had to run gas lines and beef up the electrical service, as well as a variety of other projects.

Over the past year, we had begun to use certain colors to help define our image. We were also beginning to experiment with developing our own proprietary "trade dress" to enhance our unique concept. So all told, we had quite a job in front of us to transform the space into something we could use. This was the first time we were to encounter some very real build out expenses. The landlord had made it quite clear he had no intention of helping us in any way to improve his space. That, of course, came as no surprise to us, considering the deplorable condition in which he kept his property.

We were in a quandary . . . we knew we wanted to expand our business and this seemed like the right location, but how were we going to accomplish this financially? At this point, we were a full three years old, but we were still putting every dime we made back into the business. We had decided to keep our Weston location open since our sales there covered the expenses. We really enjoyed the fact that we were now going to have two locations. We liked the way that sounded. Our new corporate goal? Total world domination.

Right when our eyebrows had twisted themselves into the deepest furrow imaginable reflecting on how we were going to get enough money to accomplish our build out, we had yet another wondrous, totally unexpected miracle happen to us. Mark's mom and dad, St. Gerald and St. LuAnn, the patron saints of entrepreneurs, came to our rescue. They had very generously decided to make an investment in KC-K9 Bakery, Inc. In exchange for their monetary investment, we gave them a small percentage of our company. The investment, while relatively small, absolutely meant the world to us. It allowed us to move comfortably into our new location, run those gas lines, paint those walls, put those deposits down on the utilities, get stocked up on labels and printed materials and perform other important tasks.

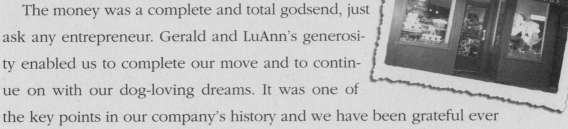

The money was a complete and total godsend, just ask any entrepreneur. Gerald and LuAnn's generosity enabled us to complete our move and to continue on with our dog-loving dreams. It was one of the key points in our company's history and we have been grateful ever since. Of course, we realize that many entrepreneurs do not get a lucky break like this. Many entrepreneurs are able to raise investment funds by selling off a piece of their business, but our situation was a bit more precarious, making their investment a complete act of faith. Our assets were basically nil, we had no cash reserves and our balance sheet only showed three hungry dogs on the assets side. All we can say is, "Thanks for the help. We'll never forget it."

As the workmen began to overhaul our space, another great thing happened to us. We had taped paper up over the plate glass windows in front and put up temporary signs stating, COMING SOON! KC-K9 BAKERY . . . THE BAKERY FOR DOGS! (Build that excitement!) There happened to be a successful sports bar located directly across the street from our storefront and every Tuesday afternoon a very popular radio sports show was broadcast live from inside. It was a call-in show and usually featured a prominent sports figure as a guest. The host of the show was an incredibly funny guy who kept mentioning our name and speculating to his radio audience as to what we really were. "A BAKERY FOR DOGS? COME ON! YOU GOTTA BE KIDDIN' US AROUND HERE!" Each week he sprinkled references to us throughout his show, always in a funny way. It even got to where the show's listeners who called in would mention us. IT WAS GREAT! The free publicity was wonderful, as God knows we had no extra money for buying ads to tell people about our new location. Every day we would run into people who would say, "You guys sure are getting a lot of free publicity from SportsTalk!" and boy were they right! So we would like to publicly say thanks to that show's host, Al Eschbach, for giving us that early, much-needed boost.

Kansas City is a great place to be an entrepreneur. Not only are the costs of doing business low here, there is also a large labor pool available and a lot of affluence here, too. There is another reason why it's great to be an entrepreneur in Kansas City: The Kauffman Foundation Center for Entrepreneurial Leadership. The Kauffman Foundation was started by a man who became one of our nation's great entrepreneurs, Ewing Kauffman. He started his pharmaceutical company, Marion Laboratories, out of his garage and thirty years later, it was enjoying sales revenues well in excess of a billion dollars annually. He became a great civic leader and inspirational benefactor to our city.

Today his great work continues on through his foundation. Entrepreneurs from all over the country flock to the Kauffman Foundation, as it has developed into quite the hotbed for entrepreneurial activity. In fact, the best money we ever spent as a company was the tuition we paid to participate in a course called the FastTrac program, developed by Courtney Price, Ph.D. She is a dynamic and charismatic woman and a very successful entrepreneur in her own right. Over the course of a semester, this unique program walked us, step by step, through the creation of our company's own business plan. In order to graduate, you had to have completed a comprehensive business plan, a useful and important tool for any business.

Each class was devoted to a different aspect of developing a business. What made the FastTrac program so valuable, though, was that there were approximately thirty-five other entrepreneurs in the class to help share experiences and observations. Many times one of our classmates would share something with the rest of us that would end up saving everyone time, money or aggravation. There were also weekly guest speakers who were successful entrepreneurs.

One evening our class spent quite a bit of time discussing proprietary concepts and how best to protect your rights to your own business ideas. We also talked about "corporate spies" and the lengths that people will go to in order to steal other people's ideas. The guest speaker that night was a man who had started his company baking cinnamon rolls in his kitchen and had, in five years, parlayed his yummy desserts into a national chain of 270 franchised bakeries called T. J. Cinnamon's with annual revenues of $70 million. He told all of us budding entrepreneurs horror story after horror story of what we could expect if our ideas hit. We all sat there staring at him, mesmerized, with our hackles standing on end and our teeth bared. I could remember thinking, "Hmmm, I wonder if he's just paranoid or what?" (Now that we've witnessed firsthand the incredible and desperate lengths that people will go to in order to steal our idea, the answer is clearly no, he wasn't being paranoid.)

I hate to admit it, but with thoughts of corporate spies drifting though our brains, we began to view people with a bit more suspicion. "Hmmmm . . . why did she ask what time we opened?" "Hmmmm . . .why did he ask what flavors we bake our cakes?" "Hmmmm . . .why is that person just standing there, looking into our bakery cases?" Well, of course, now WE were the ones being paranoid and we quickly discovered that we did not like it. We decided that we wouldn't worry about spies, but we agreed that if someone ever did spy or steal our ideas, we would be ruthless in protecting our rights. We had just worked too darn hard to feel any other way.

Having said all that, you can imagine our level of suspicion when early

Peek-A-Poo Pretzels

1 1/2 cups whole wheat flour   1/4 cup vegetable shortening
1/4 cup honey   4 tablespoons iced water   1/2 cup peanuts, chopped

Preheat oven to 300 degrees. Combine flour, honey and shortening until crumbly. Add iced water, one tablespoon at a time, until mixture binds together. Knead until smooth. Cut into 8 equal portions. Roll each portion between the hands into a strip 12 inches long by 1/2 inch thick. Shape into pretzel form. Place on a baking sheet sprayed with a nonstick cooking spray. Spritz pretzels with water and sprinkle with chopped peanuts. Bake for 25 minutes. Pretzels will harden as they cool on pan. Store in a sealed container. Yield: 8 pretzels.

the following week, Mark and I noticed a man wandering about inside our bakery. He seemed to be there a long, long time. He spent a good deal of time studying our displays, going from shelf to shelf looking at our product names and looking into our bakery cases. We knew he was a corporate spy and was more than likely using some sort of hidden camera to record our secrets. We had to act—fast! Should I tackle him? Call 911? Grab his briefcase, with the hidden camera, and run? Finally, we decided just to confront him.

"Hi! Can we help you find anything?" Mark asked brightly.

I was watching from a distance, ready to spring into action if he sprayed Mace into Mark's face and bolted.

"Yes, I believe you can," he replied. "Are you the owner of this place?"

"I am one of the owners and Dan, back there, is the other. What can we do for you today?" Mark responded.

When I saw them both looking at me, I laid down my rolling pin, relaxed my Spybuster expression and waved a friendly greeting.

He continued, "Listen. I think your bakery is a fabulous idea. I don't know how you came up with this idea, but I'd love to hear the story. I think you two are sitting on a gold-mine. Let me introduce myself. My name is Richard Gibson and I am a reporter for The Wall Street Journal. I would love to share your story with the world. If I told you I wanted to break a story on you this Thursday, would you agree not to talk to any other reporters between now and then?"

Gee, that was going to be tough. Of course, with straight faces, we agreed that we would try to keep all the reporters at bay until Thursday. Hahahaha. Of course we would agree to that! It wasn't as if journalists were beating down the door to get to us.

This was great! We agreed to his request and set a time when we could be interviewed. He seemed like a really nice guy. The interview was brief but detailed. We were terribly excited about the prospect of being in *The Wall Street Journal*. Then, true to his word and before we knew it, his funny story appeared that Thursday on the front page of the Marketplace section of the *Journal*. The headline read, Some Of The Puns Are Half-Baked, And The Place Is Going To The Dogs. Needless to say, the phone was ringing off the hook as we unlocked our door that day and we swear it didn't stop ringing for weeks afterward. Yet another miracle in our lives. Thanks God! And thank you, Richard Gibson, wherever you are!

THE WALL STREET JOURNAL.

MARKETPLACE

Some of the Puns Are Half-Baked, And the Place Is Going to the Dogs

By RICHARD GIBSON
Staff Reporter of THE WALL STREET JOURNAL

KANSAS CITY, Mo. — At the KC K9 bakery for dogs, it's all bone appetit!

For starters, there are six varieties of fresh-baked dog biscuits — peanut butter, oatmeal raisin, honey granola, coconut almond, carob chip and vegetable beef. (They're $3.99 a pound, but for the voracious, 10-pound bags are also available.) Bone-shaped biscuits too mundane? How about those that look like mini cheese pizzas, or barbecued ribs? Other treats include yogurt-filled sandwich cookies, petit fours and something called doggie doughnuts. Not to mention birthday cakes in carrot, banana or carob-chip flavors, and smaller versions called Pupcakes.

This is purebread stuff. All items are made without preservatives, sodium, sugar or fillers sometimes found in national-brand dog biscuits. Another difference: The treats don't smell — or taste — like ordinary dog food.

"We are not health-nut fanatics," owners Mark Beckloff and Dan Dye say in a brochure designed to convince skeptics, "but we are concerned as both dog lovers and dog owners about what we feed our ... girls." Their "girls" are Sarah, a Dalmatian, and Gra-

cie, a Great Dane.

The KC K9's fare is solely for dogs. Indeed, customers are invited to bring their pooches. And their puns, The owners, for instance, are thinking about a line of Great Danish. Other artful possibilities: beagles with cream cheese, blueberry mutt-ins, puppyseed rolls and pound cake. All made, of course, with Fidough.

A few critics have growled about the whole idea of a bakery for dogs. Mr. Beckloff says, adding: "People with cats think we discriminate against them. We don't — but cats are so finicky."

One customer barked up the wrong treat. Mr. Beckloff recalls the woman who came in for a cake she'd ordered for "Norma." What kind of dog is Norma, he asked. "Oh, she's not a dog," the woman replied. "A friend then? What breed does Norma have?" Mr. Beckloff inquired. "Norma doesn't have a dog," the puzzled woman replied. At which point Mr. Beckloff thought he had better ask why she was buying a cake for a dog.

The woman looked horrified. "Oh, no!" she said, explaining that she and a friend had stopped in recently and purchased some heart-shaped cookies to eat at the movies. They liked them so much they decided to order a cake.

Chapter 8

Barking Up the Right Tree

We just didn't realize what it meant to be featured in *The Wall Street Journal*. We had been very excited thinking about the story, but we hadn't thought it all the way through to its logical conclusion. Plus, it had all come about so quickly. If there was one downside to this exciting opportunity, it was that the story was to break at the start of our incredibly busy Christmas season. It made us really nervous about our ability to bake fast enough. Christmas has always been our busiest time of the year, when the demand for our wholesome treats totally outstrips our ability to produce them. At any

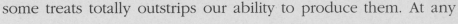

rate, this was our first Christmas that we were actually located in a real retail environment so we knew we were going to be extra busy.

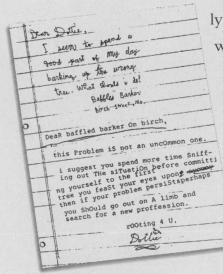

Dear Dottie,

I seem to spend a good part of my day barking up the wrong tree. What should I do?

Baffled Barker
Birch Street, Mo.

Dear baffled barker on birch,

this Problem is not an uncommon one. I suggest you spend more time sniffing out The situation before committing yourself to the first tree you feast your eyes upon. perhaps then if your problem persists you should go out on a limb and search for a new proffession.

rooting 4 U,
Dottie

Once the story did break, our phone lines (we had two) became so overloaded that many times over the next few days, they simply went dead. The first time it happened, we dashed over to use our neighbor's phone to call the phone company to get us back up again. No one could figure out why the phone would suddenly go dead in the middle of a phone order. We were frantic. We had to get those lines working again! Finally, a representative was able to explain that even with their split-second circuitry, the volume of calls was such that the incoming calls could not be rerouted fast enough and it was causing our lines to go dead.

"FIX IT!—NOW!" we barked into the receiver! Save your lame excuses! Get our lines working again! There are hungry dogs out there waiting for our treats! My God, this was our one-shot chance to take advantage of being in *The Wall Street Journal* and we were intoxicated with power and fame! (Thank you, Richard Gibson. Thank you, Richard Gibson. Thank you, Richard Gibson) Nice, nice people with friendly, laughing voices were calling us from all over the country, requesting information, flyers, biscuits, anything they could get their paws on. As a company, we still didn't have much in the way of any promotional literature with which to tell our story. What little we did have was often fairly crummy, homemade pieces that I had put together on my computer at work. However, we did take consolation from the fact that at least they were honest and accurate and were written straight from the heart.

Mark, sniffing out an opportunity, jumped in and immediately put together a sales plan to capitalize on all our calls. He is so great about stuff like that. I've never met anyone who can react so quickly to almost any situation. Before an hour had gone by, he had transformed our call-taking from, "Yes, we'll send you a flyer about our company right away" to "Yes, that's right. We have a great value to offer you and it's available only to callers from *The Wall Street Journal*. It's a special sampler that contains our most popular bakery items along with a couple of pounds of fresh-baked biscuits. We can send that out right away." He transformed informational calls into revenue-producing sales calls. See why he's the greatest partner?

The biggest problem that Mark and I faced was that we were still hand-kneading each and every batch of biscuits. (It's always fun hearing stories from our customers who tell us they would pass by our storefront in the wee hours of the morning, when the area bars were closing, and they'd look in and see us way in the back, the kitchen lights burning brightly, still kneading dough and making biscuits for the next day.) Although we had begun to hire some additional employees to help out with the overload, we couldn't afford to pay overtime. We were probably up to seven or eight employees by this point and we could have used three times that many easily. This is often the plight of small businesses. You need people (and machines) to help you expand, but usually you need the people (and machines) before you have the revenues to support them. It seemed that no matter how much money we were making, we had so many ways to spend it to help the business grow.

So for weeks on end the phone rang. The way we answered the phone became almost a chant, a mantra:

"Thank you for calling KC-K9. This is Mark. Can you hold, please?"

"Thank you for calling KC-K9. This is Dan. Can you hold, please?"

We immediately installed another phone line to help with the overload, although we hated to spend more on our phone bill each month. We still had absolutely no system in place for doing mail orders, so you can understand our panic. While we were totally thrilled with the response we were receiving, our production capacity was still so limited that we experienced tremendous frustration.

Half of the time, we were taking names and addresses on the backs of napkins, scraps of paper, flaps of cardboard boxes, anything that was handy. I hate to reveal how stupid we really were, but after we sent out our mail orders, we would simply throw away the name! Sometimes we like to tell that story to mail-order experts just to watch their reaction. It's one of the most stupid things a company can ever do. We just assumed the people would call back when they needed more treats. How's that for confidence?! It still makes us sick to think of how many names we threw away, not realizing their importance to our company. But as they say, you live and you learn. We are still trying to get better about communicating with our customers.

THE YUMMIEST PHONE MESSAGE YOU'LL EVER TAKE.

"Please hold..."
Peanut Butter Cups

1/2 cup carob chips, unsweetened
6 teaspoons peanut butter

12 confection candy cups

Place cups on a tray that will fit in your refrigerator. In a small pan, on medium heat, melt carob chips. Spoon 1/2 teaspoon of melted carob into each cup. Chill 10 minutes. Spoon 1/2 teaspoon of peanut butter on top of chilled carob. Spoon 1/2 teaspoon of melted carob in top of peanut butter. Chill 10 minutes. Peel and treat! Store in refrigerator. Yield: 12 cups.

KEEP A STACK by the Phone...FILE LATER FOR EASY ACCESS.

At one point, our cardboard box began to overflow with biscuit orders and flyer requests. We finally put one person in charge of getting the orders out as quickly as he could. We had really reached a point where we were constantly juggling our limited production capacity to accommodate our growing needs. We had to stock our two retail bakeries, at least two hundred wholesale accounts and now our new mail-order business (which was now literally six weeks backlogged, thanks to the *WSJ* story). We were really dogpaddling! What we would have given for unlimited production capacity! The maximum amount that we could produce in a day's time seemed so small and finite. We had fabulous opportunities in front of us. We had frustrating production challenges in front of us. But all things considered, it was all too beautiful for words. We were too busy being excited about our company's future to worry. We began to notice a new swagger in the girls' trot out to the car at night. Sarah seemed to really swing her hips and Dottie's tail never stopped wagging. Even Gracie began snapping out of her shyness.

Today we can proudly proclaim that we have solved our name-capturing dilemma (yes, we now save our names) and are the proud owners of what may well be one of the strangest mailing-list databases in history. Forgive us for sounding a bit critical. You see, we mail directly to the actual dogs, when possible. And when a company is doing its shipments to thousands of customers with names like Alice Von KooKoo Hound, Bone Bandit, Snuggles, and Cleopatra . . . well, you get the picture. It really is a very odd mailing list to say the least.

Another unanticipated but great side benefit to being in the *Journal* was the media calls we began to receive. Countless radio shows from all around the country began to call and invite us to tell our story on their shows. Even *The Tonight Show* called! Twice! Some were business shows, some were more entertainment oriented, but they were all done in great humor. This naturally led to even more customer interest. Dogs' ears the country over were perking up as we told our story over the airwaves. We imagined how frustrating it would feel to be a dog and be unable to use a touch-tone phone or read a credit card number into a telephone receiver. Happily, there were obviously many dogs that were able to persuade their owners to pick up the phone and do the job for them.

By this point, both Mark and I had accomplished our original goal of working for ourselves. I had long since quit my copywriter's position and had never looked back. Although we weren't taking much money for a salary, we felt rich in that we were now our own bosses and were calling our own shots. It was great that our salaries could potentially grow in direct proportion to the amount that we were willing to work. Plus, most importantly of all, we were having fun!

Not a day went by that we didn't feel thankful that we were able to do something that brought us such joy. We were completely cognizant of how lucky we were. Since we truly did love dogs with all our hearts, this was paradise. Throughout the day we could stop what we were doing and go out into the bakery and play with visiting dogs. Every day, new puppies made their way into our lives. And it was with great pride that we watched our four-legged customers grow from being fat, cuddly little pups into mature, sleek, healthy, lovable canines.

Sarah, Dottie and Gracie felt the same way. They developed their own sets of friends and I think each of them had two or three boyfriends they were juggling. Gracie used to lure customers in off the street simply by standing in the doorway looking adorable. She looked like a big comic book character. And when the trolleys would cruise past, full of tourists, they were compelled to get off at the Westport stop, if only to go back and check out that big dog standing in the doorway.

The girls get their own mail every day from people around the country. Gracie even received a marriage proposal from a Great Dane who lived in Atlanta. Such a smooth talker! He started his lusty love letter with, "I normally do not write to girls that I haven't sniffed, but you are different." We have had to sit down with them on occasion and caution them against boys who would just love them and leave them, not to mention the gold bone-diggers, who would only see them as beautiful, single, bakery heiresses. I'm sure from time to time they have each had their secret fantasies of running off with a big unfixed male to roam the countryside, with dreams of two litters a year dancing through their heads.

There have been so, so many dogs that have helped us on our road to success. Sally, a beautiful, solid-white VERY PAMPERED German shepherd has been a great customer from day one and the girls are all quite fond of her. Then there's the awesome Henry, the Great Dane who is so striking and likes to jump up on his hind legs and bark his order directly across the bakery case. He's beautiful. And Lula! Lula Mae is a gorgeous yellow Lab princess who has appeared along with Sarah, Dottie and Gracie on many national stories about our bakery. She is such a regular customer that we have actually considered putting her mommy, Lendy, on our payroll since she's there so often. Barkin' Betty, Bingo, Buttercup, Einstein, Nasha, Winthorpe, Patsy, Spooner, Casey, Lucas and Cody and Skye, Max and Maggie, Coco Chanel, Dusty, Duke . . . so many dogs, so little time. It would be impossible to acknowledge all of our great customers here and now, but they know how much we love them.

We have sometimes wished that we had kept journals of the many experiences that we have had running our bakery for dogs. I do recall an incident when a very nice lady came in to pick up a personalized birthday cake for "Norma." As I packed her cake into a box, I made small talk and asked her what kind of dog Norma was. Immediately, the expression on her face went through a tense and swift metamorphosis. She got a horrified look on her face as she snapped, "Norma is not a dog. Norma is my friend."

"Ma'am, ahhh. Let's see. We may have a misunderstanding here." I knew that from time to time someone might come in and, oh, order a glass of milk with their SnickerPoodle, a clear sign that they did not know where they were. "You obviously did not realize that this is a bakery for dogs, did you?" I queried. I watched as her face untwisted itself out of its angry snarl.

"A bakery for dogs? I've never heard of such a thing! A bakery for what? Oh. OH! How funny! A bakery for dogs!"

We immediately both threw back our heads and roared with laughter. We laughed until tears streamed out of our eyes. Every time she realized what she had almost done, she roared anew. And I chimed in, not laughing with her, but AT her. Through the peals of laughter, she snortled, chortled, choked and guffawed her way through the story of how she had come into the bakery the previous Saturday night with her boyfriend, before catching a movie.

"We both got a yogurt-filled heart cookie. Both of us sat in the movie crunching through them thinking, God, these are really hard, but they're really good in a weird way." Then she screamed with delight again at the memory. She went on to explain that she had heard our bakery was all-natural and that we didn't use salt or sugar. So she thought the treat they had eaten was normal for that kind of bakery. "I had absolutely no idea this was a bakery only for dogs! What a great idea!" she exclaimed, as she dabbed away the tears with her handkerchief. And just to prove how great dog-loving, Bakery-For-Dogs shoppers really are, she went ahead and purchased the cake that we had personalized for Norma. (Luckily, Norma had two dogs.) But is that a great customer or what?

We know that our products have been the basis for many practical jokes over the years. We routinely get groups of snickering college kids in, barely able to keep a straight face as they order a half-dozen PupCakes.® It's great. God only knows what devious and mischievous ends our treats will meet. It has been quite the experience observing life from behind the counter of the nation's original bakery for dogs.

As we have continued to expand our bone-baking horizons, we have been fortunate indeed to have garnered some great press along the way. After *The Wall Street Journal* came *The New York Times, People* magazine, the *Today* show, *The Oprah Winfrey Show*, CNN, *The Times* of London, National "Pup-lick" Radio . . . even the *National Enquirer*! We knew our three girls were publicity hounds, but this was great! Getting our name out there through various news stories has really contributed to our growth. We have learned the power of good press and we take it very seriously. To a little company like ours it has meant the difference between life and death.

So, to every reporter who has ever written a story about us and to every editor who has approved it for publication, we warmly extend our paws to you and wish you all happy lives.

Chapter 9

Goin' Uptown

Partly as a result of all the national pup-licity we were receiving, we had begun to get inquiries from some great people interested in obtaining a KC-K9 franchise. Franchising interested us, but we didn't know the first thing about it. We liked the thought of owning a franchise company. And God knows it was easy for us to visualize hundreds, thousands, MILLIONS of KC-K9 Bakeries across this great land of ours. We loved thinking that our wholesome treats could soon be available to every dog in America. As this book goes to press, we have had close to two thousand serious franchise inquiries.

But the further we got into it, the more we realized that franchising is a very intense proposition. It's like starting and running a whole second business. It also brought home to us (again) the painful fact of our limited production capacity. At the same time, it became essential to develop a central distribution system from which we could service a franchise organization. Our growth as a company would forever be stunted until we solved our production and distribution challenges.

Although we didn't have enough money to solve all our production dilemmas, we took some bold steps to begin remedying the situation. We began to look around in earnest for a baking commissary that would enable us to do some major baking. Our search was not an easy one, especially with Sarah, Dottie and Gracie sticking their big heads out all the car windows, obstructing our views of all the good real estate. We needed a building with office space as well as production space. We needed the right kind of electrical and gas service. We needed parking to accommodate our employees. And for crying out loud, could we please finally have A LOADING DOCK!? Carrying in over a ton of ingredients each week on our shoulders was getting really, really, REALLY old after doing it for four years. Not one of our locations over the years had ever come with a loading dock.

After a two- or three-month search, we found a great space in downtown Kansas City that would accommodate our baking demands. It had the right kind of power, it had parking, and it had one very big, very sweet loading dock. Most importantly, the back and the side of the building were securely fenced, so the girls could play and frolic between their numerous naps and serious snacking sessions. Once we had a central baking commissary, we were able to look around for another retail location.

We felt fat, dumb and happy after three years in our Westport location. We had grown very comfortable there. Yet we knew that our franchise stores would function best when situated in a certain, select type of retail environment, and Westport clearly did not match that profile. Our Westport store was really an oddball location; we felt we needed to develop a more "prototypical" retail site. By doing this, we could really put our retail concept to the test and develop the systems necessary to successfully operate our franchise company.

We were very excited to begin franchising our concept, but before we could even consider accepting a dime from anyone in franchise fees, we had to thoroughly learn and understand each and every detail of our retail operations. We had to open our own "model" store in an area that would demographically match the locations our franchisees would be looking for around the country. This would give us an accurate view of what a typical franchisee could expect. Without that kind of intense intimate knowledge, how could we guarantee the success of each and every franchisee? Although we felt in our hearts that we would always be doing the right thing for our franchisees, we have learned it always helps to collect as much data as you can and analyze it fully. If we could not, with 110 percent conviction, ensure success for every person who wanted to team up with us, then the process would not be worth it.

The only place we could seriously look for a prototype store location in Kansas City was our famed Country Club Plaza shopping district. Known simply as "The Plaza" to Kansas Citians, it is home to such upscale retailers as Saks Fifth Avenue, Eddie Bauer, The Bath and Body Shop, Tivol's Jewels and generations of the top names in exclusive Kansas City retailing. Many of the city's finest restaurants are located on the Plaza. Now it would be home to the greatest and most famous shop of them all:

THREE DOG BAKERY! THE BAKERY FOR DOGS!

Meanwhile, as we began to negotiate our Plaza lease, we wanted to get the ball rolling on all the legal work that franchising would en"tail." This way we could be ready to sell when we felt we had learned enough. We consulted with several franchising experts and began to school ourselves on what it took to become a franchise organization. We hired a tremendously knowledgeable franchise attorney along with a great franchise adviser who had a proven track record. Franchising is not a cheap program to develop, let us assure you! It costs a lot of money to produce all the legal documentation that a company needs before it can even *begin* the selling process.

get the Tuna Balls Rollin'

3 cups cake flour

1 medium egg

3 tablespoons cornmeal

1 6-ounce can of tuna packed in water, drained

1/4 cup Parmesan cheese

2 teaspoons oregano

1 tablespoon vegetable oil

3/4 cup water

Preheat oven to 350 degrees. Combine all dry ingredients. Add wet ingredients and mix well. Roll into quarter-size balls between the hands. Place on baking sheet sprayed with a nonstick cooking spray. Bake for 30 minutes. Cool on baking sheet. Should still be soft after cooling. Store in a sealed container. Yield: 24 balls.

As long as we were determined to develop our new franchise anchor store, we decided it would be the perfect time to finally go ahead and change our name. If you will recall, a few chapters back we discussed the problems and challenges we had faced with "KC-K9 Bakery." After discussing the pros and cons of dozens of potential names and after much thinking and soul-searching, we decided, for a variety of reasons, to use **Three Dog Bakery**. We would continue to use **The Bakery For Dogs** as our sell line. The girls loved the new name and they showed their appreciation by eating even more treats than before.

We were becoming enormously enthusiastic about the prospect of franchising, and we began to meet incredibly exciting and creative people who wanted to be part of our concept. This was and *is* unbelievably flattering to Mark and me. We began to mentally handpick the franchise candidates who we felt would be easy to work with, who shared our passion for dogs and who believed in our company's mission and vision. Potential franchisees were approaching us with some very creative ideas. All of a sudden it hit us that we would probably learn as much from our franchisees as they would learn from us!

It is important to both Mark and me, as our little company grows, that we carefully control the quality of our treats. Growing up to be a huge company would be no fun to us whatsoever if it meant compromising the high quality of our ingredients or formulations. We have always tried to hire nice people who share our vision and who can see the merits of baking fabulous treats for dogs. This philosophy has served us well over the years, and we have had very little employee turnover as a result.

We ended up spending a couple of months completely gutting and remodeling our new location. When we finally got our bakery opened on the Plaza, we decided to have a blowout Grand Opening celebration. The girls wore sparkling debutante gowns with matching hats, designed especially for them by a fantastically talented seamstress. The bakery was flooded with lights in preparation for the grand event. Engraved invitations were sent out, and people jetted in from all parts of the country to participate in the gala. Dogs the city over quivered with excitement. There would be bone-bones! And chilled, sparkling water! There would be lots of paw-shaking and intriguing canine-versation—and *tail-wagging* galore! And then, to make this the absolute total social event of the season, our four-legged guests would be able to meet the legendary Sarah, Dottie and Gracie! The famed founders of the bakery created especially for canines! Lucky was the dog who held an invitation to this party in his paws! There were even cats prepared to disguise themselves as dogs in order to come, we are told.

At last, the long-awaited night arrived. The street was blocked off as the crowd grew larger and larger. The anticipation was unbearable. Electricity was in the air. Dogs were arriving dressed to the nines. Top hats and sparkling collars were the order of the day. Much, much too soon, our supply of two hundred bone bow ties ran out. All of Kansas City's television stations sent camera crews. The newspapers sent reporters. When Sarah, Dottie and Gracie dramatically arrived, fashionably late, in their stretch limousine, the crowd and the paparazzi went wild. A red carpet was laid out, guarded by the K9 security patrol and the rescued greyhounds from the Greyhound Club of Kansas City. With spectators pushing and shoving, flashbulbs popping and dogs straining on their leashes to get a better view, the girls hopped out of the limo and pranced glamorously down the red carpet. But wait—there was more! Prints of Sarah's little black paw, Dottie's little spotted paw and Gracie's mammoth white paw would be enshrined, for canine eternity, in cement outside of our bakery's entrance. The crowd loved it, and the girls did, too. Many hours later, when the festivities began to wind down and the last case of champagne had been emptied, the girls watched as the last little guest happily trotted away with his human parents, his little tail straight up in the air, wagging furiously. Today the girls little pawprints are still on view at our Plaza location, and dogs from all over the world come to gaze lovingly at them.

One of our favorite moments since we started Three Dog Bakery occurred at about this time. Not too long after our grand Grand Opening celebration, we were invited to appear on *The Oprah Winfrey Show*. Imagine the thrill! Oprah! The girls' tails immediately went into full throttle when her producer called. They were coming down to Kansas City to film our operations, and then Mark and I would be flown to Chicago to actually appear on her show. Her producer explained to us that our business would be exposed to over forty million viewers. After we picked ourselves up from the floor, we joyously did the Oprah dance, with the girls all joining in, barking hysterically. What a great opportunity!

The camera crew came down as promised and filmed our retail bakery operations, our commissary, our offices . . . and then one little surprise.

When they finished the day's filming, they unexpectedly requested to come to our house to film! Embarrassing! You see, although we are getting better, let's just say that Mark and I are not the world's best housekeepers. For the first four years of our company's development we didn't take salaries. We had no money for a maid or for buying anything nice. Or for general upkeep and maintenance. All in all, our charming turn-of-the-century house looked pretty seedy.

They weren't kidding about coming over, either. They were dead set on filming at our house . . . you know, showing the successful entrepreneurs at home. Ha! We panicked. Nobody on earth lives the way we do. I rushed home, arriving only minutes before the film crew. I tore through the house like a cyclone, kicking clothes, papers, dog hair and debris under the couch, inside drawers, under rugs . . . anyplace I could find. I cursed under my breath, lamenting the fact that we lived like swine. Before we started the bakery, we actually had dignity and pride . . . and a housekeeper.

Mercifully, their filming was brief and superficial. They assured us that the condition of our house was exactly what they were hoping to find. The show's theme that day was on how successful entrepreneurs often do *not* live the millionaire playboy lifestyle. Good God, if that's what they were looking for, we were classic examples. Surprisingly though, after the miracle of editing, the old homestead didn't look too bad when the show aired. The Oprah crew deserves an Emmy Award for Best Editing for that one.

When we flew to Chicago to be on the show, it was terrifically exciting and great fun. Oprah is every bit as nice off camera as she is on. Not only did she pay our airfares, but she also paid for a very plush, first-rate hotel suite, stretch limos and a generous dining allowance. WE LOVE YOU, OPRAH! Plus, to make her perfect, she *loves* dogs. She brings her two cute cocker spaniels to work with her every day and has a herd of golden retrievers at her farm. You gotta love that. Oprah's the best in our eyes. Being on her show brought us a ton of new business. Thanks, Oprah!

Time has rolled on, and with it have come even more super exciting opportunities for our hard-workin' little company. Just as we were getting down to the final details of our franchise program, we received a call that would once again change our lives.

Chapter 10
No Time to Paws

Both Mark and I agree that one of the great attractions of running our own company is the amazing range of experiences it has offered us. Whether we are learning about baking equipment, marketing opportunities or employee issues, this rich diversity has made our lives full of excitement and challenges. We never know what each day will bring. Some days we have gone to work just feeling like, Ho-hum, here's another day, and then out of nowhere we will get a call from—who knows? *People* magazine! The *Today* show! And our whole day will change directions. We love that! One of the most depressing thoughts we could ever have is that our lives would settle down into a predictable, routine pattern. Maybe we shouldn't admit it, but we both thrive on change and the chaos that ensues.

We try to stay open to any and all opportunities that may arise. This is a trait that we have desperately tried to instill into all our associates. Early in January 1996, our day screeched to a very exciting halt when we received **THE CALL.** The voice, while pleasant, was deep and resonant and was shrouded with mystery. Speaking slowly and succinctly, The Voice proceeded to announce that it was representing the world's largest chain of pet superstores, Phoenix-based PETsMART. I sucked in my breath and my heart started to pound. The Voice wanted to know if there was any interest on our part in forming a partnership with PetsMart to bring our unique concept and great treats to their superstores. The next thing I remember after regaining consciousness was scraping myself up off the floor and gasping into the phone, "Of course we're interested! Yes, of course, we're interested. How? When? Where?"

It was any entrepreneur's dream come true . . . teaming up with a big corporation that would help your company grow and help you realize your dreams. We agreed to speak again in a few days, and I hung up and dashed out to our baking area to tell Mark, who was supervising at the ovens. After he passed out and was revived, we rushed in to call our trusted longtime friend, Bill Reisler. Our relationship with Bill has been all-encompassing and of utmost importance to us. In fact, his role in our company as adviser/investor/mentor has been so instrumental to our success that it is truly a subject for a whole other book. His advice is always thought-provoking, and he has a great talent for helping us to see the big picture. Mark and I usually do not do anything significant without first consulting him.

To say that we were intensely excited doesn't even scratch the surface of what we were feeling. Bill was extremely positive and as excited as we were by this new turn of events. As promised, The Voice called back in a few days, and we arranged to meet with the PetsMart executives at their corporate headquarters in Phoenix later in the month.

If we were optimistic about working out a deal with PetsMart in those first few days, that feeling only intensified when Bill compiled a five-inch stack of information for us about the company. Wow! **What a great company!** PetsMart is an incredibly well-run, billion-dollar public corporation with a highly regarded and well-respected management team. It seemed as though every major investment house in the country was recommending

PetsMart stock as a Strong Buy. They are aggressive in their growth, yet they are passionate about community-mindedness. Their corporate goals are meshed with a bold spirit of social consciousness, which we found to be very refreshing.

Mark and I have often admired companies that go about their good deeds in a quiet way. Besides offering employment opportunities to tens of thousands of Americans, PetsMart finds homes for tens of thousands of lovable homeless pets through their in-store pet adoption centers. We love that. PetsMart puts its money where its mouth is.

The more we learned about PetsMart, the more we began to feel that this would not be a run-of-the-mill business deal. This had the potential to be a powerful relationship, one that we could feel proud to be a part of. A caring, gererous attitude like PetsMart's can truly bring about great changes in our society. It is very exciting to finally see more companies assuming and accepting responsibility for bettering the planet. And all of us, as cash-paying consumers, need to exercise our influence and demand this type of corporate behavior from all the companies with which we do business. Think of the ripple effect!

We were scheduled to meet on January 23, 1996 . . . a day that will live in history. One little detail that we had forgotten was the Super Bowl, which was taking place in Phoenix that weekend. Reservations clerks the city over laughed in our face as we tried to find a hotel room, and we barely managed to rent a car. But we finally made it, and we were very honored to have the opportunity to meet Mark Hansen, the president of PetsMart, Don Dorsey, the chief financial officer, and Ron Butler, the executive vice president of marketing. Our meeting lasted two or three hours. They got a chance to look at us up close, and vice versa. It was scary and fun and thrilling all at the same time.

We talked about Three Dog Bakery, our past, the present and what our dreams were for the future. They talked about PetsMart and where they were headed. To tell you the truth, we felt a little awed by the fact that PetsMart is also very much an entrepreneurial company. In fact, they aren't much older than we are. If that doesn't illustrate the power of assembling a great team when growing a business, then nothing does. In just a little more time than we had been in business, they had already managed to go public, open stores in three hundred high-profile locations, hire thousands and become a billion-dollar company. Excuse me while I wipe away a tear of jealousy. Nothing like a little reality check to keep you humble.

*one (BIG) potato PIE

1 large sweet potato
1/4 cup honey

1 medium egg
1 1/2 cups white flour

1/4 cup vegetable shortening
3 tablespoons iced water
1 8-inch pie pan

Preheat oven to 350 degrees. Cook sweet potato for approximately 1 hour, until soft. (Note: Leave oven on at 350; same temperature required to bake pie.) Peel and mix with 1/8 cup honey and the egg. To make pie crust, combine flour, remaining honey and shortening until crumbly. Add iced water one tablespoon at a time until mixture binds together. Knead until smooth. Roll out and press crust into pans. Pour sweet potato mixture into crust. Bake for 40 minutes until sweet potato mixture is set. Place pie while still in pan on a rack to cool. Cover with plastic wrap. Yield: 1 pie.

I, SARAH, PROMISE to eat the WHOLE pie and NOTHIN' but the whole p

We left our meeting floating on cloud nine—er, cloud canine. In fact, we found we didn't even need our airline tickets home, as we floated the entire way. The PetsMart executives were not intimidating at all. They graciously made us feel right at home. That spoke volumes to us about why they are so successful as a company. You can't grow the way they're growing without being good people.

Over the next several months we worked out the details of our partnership. The timing was perfect. PetsMart was planning to open five hot new concept stores, and Three Dog Bakery was going to be a part of them. We couldn't have been happier to hear that the market they were going to open these stores in was SAN DIEGO! Yes! Please keep in mind that we are from Kansas. The blowing wind, the endless prairies, the biggest event of our day was watching the cloud of dust kicked up by an old pickup truck as it rumbled past. So just stop and fantasize with us for a moment as we relish the beauty, the glamour, the jet-set allure of SAN DIEGO! The sun, the surf, the total heaven of **SAN DIEGO**! What if the next market they had chosen to open in had been—well, I won't say in case you live there. But you can imagine what might easily have been. Remember a few chapters back when we talked about our Guardian Angel? See what we mean?

PetsMart had already set Grand Opening dates of May 28, 1996, for their San Diego stores, so we had a lot of catching up to do. With great urgency, we laid our stores out, designed them, ordered equipment, determined our model line of merchandise and flew to California to hire our bakery employees. We promoted one of our employees, John Escalada, to market manager of this exciting new Three

PETsMART
Where pets are family.

Dog territory. Our head pastry chef, Patricia Berlau, eagerly accepted the challenge of going to San Diego to train the new in-store bakers. It was all coming together.

It certainly was no small task pulling five bakeries together at the same time, not only for the usual reasons, but also because they were located 1,700 miles away. Dottie, Sarah and Gracie were eager to see the new bakeries, and they felt as nervous as we did. They kept asking if they were famous yet. This was the first time that we had ventured outside of the Kansas City area with our retail bakery. Even though we were enjoying a howling success with our mail-order business, we were curious to see if our retail success was merely a Kansas City "local-boys-make-good" phenomenon.

The big day eventually arrived. The new pastry chefs were trained, the shelves were stocked, signs were in place and we were ready. Our three girls, bedecked in jeweled gowns with matching pillbox hats, made a personal appearance all the way from KC. They arrived at the Murphy Canyon PetsMart store by chauffer-driven stretch limosine. Other celebridogs arrived in separate limos, including Eddie, the cute, talented terrier on TV's *Frasier*. Their grand Hollywood-style entrance would have made Lassie *and* Rin Tin Tin proud.

We are happy to report that the PetsMart stores are everything we hoped they would be. Designed with the help of a world-class, internationally renowned design firm, these fabulous forty-thousand-square-foot pet palaces set new industry standards. Anything your pet needs or desires can be found somewhere down these aisles. Exotic saltwater fish? They got 'em. Hand-stitched leather horse saddles? They got 'em. Complete one-stop shopping for dogs, cats, fish, birds, lizards, hamsters . . . you name it. Veterinary

IF YOU'LL JUST FOLLOW ME MAAM....

clinic, a groomer, a photography studio, an equestrian department—it's all there. The stores are unbelievable. At the top of the heap is the stunning jewel in the crown: Three Dog Bakery. (Of course, our opinion is just a bit biased.)

Since the stores have opened, Mark and I have spent a great deal of time

talking to our new customers at the five bakeries: in Chula Vista, Oxnard, El Cajon, Vista and San Diego. We have been delighted at how warmly Three Dog Bakery has been received. It answered our question about whether Three Dog Bakery was just a Kansas City thing. It's clearly a people-who-love-dogs thing. We are genuinely and deeply touched by the response. It has renewed our spirit.

As our first sales reports are starting to trickle in, Mark and I are again stopping to reflect. We are taking stock of where Three Dog Bakery has come from and where it is going. How fortunate we are to live in a great country—a country civilized enough to unabashedly revel in the joys of its pets. It is clearly time for us to count the many, many blessings this life has bestowed upon us. It took a lot of hard work to get here, and it will take even harder work in the years to come to stay on top of it all.

Business, by its very nature, is nothing more that a combination of people coming together and creating something where there was once nothing. We've seen businesses come and go around us. We've seen people's lives ruined by greed and bad choices. But we have also seen lives enriched and empowered by hard work and creative visualization. We have been touched by thousands of generous souls along our way, and we can only hope that we have touched those souls back.

Please indulge us, for just a moment, while we become philosophical. If being in business for ourselves has taught us anything, it has been that life is very sweet and precious and so very fleeting. That may seem like quite an observation to come out of a simple book about a bakery for dogs. But over the last six years we feel like we have been through an emotional wringer. We have experienced the highest of highs and the lowest of lows. Our personal lives have been closely intertwined with our business.

Yet it is because of this emotional roller-coaster ride that we have started to understand and appreciate what work really means. It is a constant in life. Work is truly its own reward. When you are able to push aside all the day-to-day pettiness and distractions and just focus on being the best that you can be, work becomes a wondrous thing. It no longer is some-thing you dread or feel that you have to do. It's something you look forward to. (Jeez, I never thought I'd say that.) Everyone can experience work in that way, not just business owners. If everyone everywhere just concentrated and focused on doing their absolute best, all the rest would take care of itself. If  you are strong enough and brave enough to follow your true heart's desire, and if you do your absolute, passionate best and believe in yourself, you'll achieve everything that you want. It sounds so shockingly simple, but it's true. We've seen it time and time again with ourselves and with others. If any of that rings true with you, we wish you good luck on your journey. We wish you twice the success that we've had. Go for your dream! Go for it!

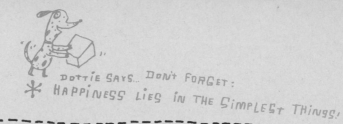

Simply Sumptuous Fruit Cubes

1 12-ounce can frozen fruit juice, unsweetened
3 ice cube trays

Add water to juice per instructions on can, pour into trays, freeze and serve.
If your dog loves to crunch on ice cubes, this is a grrreat surprise treat!
(Outdoor cube eating is recommended.)

It's so simple...

We hope that you have enjoyed reading our short "tail." We are living proof that anyone can make it. Not that we have "made" it (whatever that means), but if we were to go belly-up tomorrow, we would both feel that we had accomplished something worthwhile, and that, in some small way, we really had made some sort of contribution, at least to a lot of happy dogs. And for us, it will always come back to dogs. That's what we're all about. We know 'em. We love 'em. We can't live without 'em.

As a final thought, I am reminded of a happy little story that occurred not long after we opened our bakery in Westport. It was getting to be closing time and not much was going on in the bakery. Mark and I were getting the place cleaned up and restocked for the next day. At about ten minutes till nine, a man came into the bakery with a very cute but *very* cranky little boy who was about five years old. It must have been past his bedtime.

Anyway, this little boy was whining and crying and pulling at his dad's trousers. The dad was being extremely patient and was trying to coax his son out of his mood. But to anything his dad said or asked him, the little boy would just scream "NO!" in reply. I was trying to soothe him, too, by asking him if he had ever been to a bakery for dogs before. "Wwwwaaaaaa!" was his answer.

Suddenly big ol' Gracie, who had been snooping around for last-minute treats, lumbered out from behind the bakery counter. Being deaf, she had not heard the boy and his dad come in, and when she rounded the corner, the looks on her face *and* the little boy's were priceless. A photographer could have snapped a prize-winning photo at that moment. He immediately stopped crying, and his eyes widened with a mixture of fear and wonder. Children always relate and bond with Gracie. I don't know if they think she's a cartoon character or what. She's such a striking—yet sweet—big, big dog. Fortunately, she loves children, too.

Gracie slowly approached the little boy, her huge padded paws shuffling over the floor. The little boy held tightly to his daddy's leg. I knelt down and introduced him to Gracie.

"Would you like to pet her?" I asked. "She's nice. And she's about five years old, too." He mumbled an unintelligible reply.

"Go ahead. Pet her. She's a Great Dane," his father explained.

Once more the boy mumbled some sort of response, but after seeing his dad petting Gracie, he reluctantly extended his arm to touch her. Then he did it again. And again. Within a few moments, he was all over her. Petting her head, lifting her paws, hugging her neck and trying to give her a kiss.

"Can we have a Great Dane?" he was now asking.

I silently watched them as they touched Gracie and Gracie touched them. After a few minutes, the tantrum forgotten, they headed for the door hand-in-hand, all smiles. I followed them to the door and said good night, preparing to lock the door after them. The last thing I heard as the door banged shut was the little boy telling his dad, "I feel better now that I've petted a dog!"

That is the magic of dogs.

Wagging Tails, Cold Wet Noses and Warm Licks

On behalf of everyone here at Three Dog Bakery, we just wanted to say a heartfelt **"THANKS"** to everyone who bought this book. We really appreciate it. It was fun to write it and to relive all the old memories again. Sarah, Dottie and Gracie send you their best, too, and look forward to personally shaking paws with all of you in the future.

We don't know where the future will take our little company. We know we want to keep growing and following our mission, which is **to bake the best dog treats on the planet and to get them to as many dogs as possible**. We know that no one in life makes it on his own. We all get help, no matter what it is that we do, from other sources, directly and indirectly. I think we've made it pretty clear throughout this book that we have had lots of assistance on our journey.

Obviously, we would not be in business today were it not for our **great retail customers** (who happen to be the best customers in the world). So many of you have stuck with us from the very beginning, and all we can do is worship you and grovel at your feet in thanksgiving. Please join us in giving yourselves a big round of applause. Thanks, too, to all of our **wholesale accounts**. Because of you guys, we are able to sell our treats in places all over the country, which has really helped us get known. Your advice and support have been the backbone of our company. Thanks so much.

It would be an impossible task to even try to thank everyone who has contributed in some way to our story. But certainly some special thanks are in order:

Special thanks to Bill Reisler and the Kansas City Equity Partners. We met Bill several years ago through his charming and funny wife, Vicky, who was one of our customers. Mere words could never adequately express what his advice and support have meant to our company. He was one of the first to encourage us to "get out there." He serves as a Three Dog Bakery board member and investor. In fact, we have been able to accomplish some of our dreams because of his financial support. Bill has been a longtime supporter of Kansas City businesses, and without his invigorating presence, Kansas City would be a much bleaker place. He has been a constant source of inspiration for us, and his work and dedication touch many, many lives. Thanks, Bill, for everything. We're glad to know you and all of the associates at KCEP.

Special thanks to Ann Willoughby and the Willoughby Design Group. Have you ever met someone who enriches your life, just by knowing her? That is Ann to us. She is a beautiful woman with a beautiful spirit. She is an incredibly talented designer and incredibly nice and positive person. We first met her at our little bakery in Weston. She came in with her son and her husband, and after being in the shop for two minutes, she came up to our counter and said, "You guys . . . this is a wonderful place. This is a hundred-million-dollar concept and I'd love to help take you there." You gotta love that. Ann's client roster reads like a veritable Who's Who of the nation's business world. She's simply the best. She is one the many angels that have touched our business and our lives. Without Ann Willoughby, Three Dog Bakery would not be the place it is today. Thanks, Annie!

Special thanks to our mommies and daddies. A special thanks to Mark's mom and dad, for being incredibly supportive and interested from the very, very beginning. Thanks to LuAnn for giving Mark the bone cutter in his Christmas stocking, which set this whole thing off. LuAnn's daily calls to check on how sales were going during those early days became an important motivator for us. We appreciate all the support! Thanks for believing in us! And a special thanks to my dad, Virgil, for teaching me to love all animals and to my mom, Annetta, who would not have cared what I did with my life, as long as I was happy.

Special thanks to Meg Cundiff and all her beautiful hair. Meg's contribution to our company, like her hair, has been enormous. She is one of the most in-demand artists working today, and we are darn, and I do mean DARN, lucky that she makes time to squeeze our requests in. Meg was the first person who was able to give our company the personality that we wanted it to have, through her artwork. She *always* knows the right thing to do. If there is one thing that we are regularly complimented on (besides our great treats, of course) it is the artwork that Meg provides for our company. She's crazy, she's koo-koo and she sometimes frightens us, but that's exactly why we love her. She's funny, she's nice and we are incredibly lucky to know her. Thanks, Meggy! We hereby nominate you (and your hair) for Best Artist of the Century. XOXOXO

Special Thanks to Gail & Richard Lozoff. Talk about your successful entrepreneurs! Jeez Louise! Gail & Richard's chain of wildly successful Bagel & Bagel restaurants have set new industry standards. They've grown from one neighbrohood location in KC to national expansion under their new name of Einsteins. Gail, you go, girl! Their roles as friends, great advice givers, and inventors could never be repaid.

Special thanks to <u>Andrews and McMeel</u>. Writing this book has definitely been the funnest, most exciting thing that we have done. Especially when the publisher happens to be the world's number one humor publisher! Thanks for providing the planet with so much fun and laughter. The most special thanks to Jean Lowe, our editor, who has been so nice and patient. . . refusing to yell at us no matter how late we turned in our chapters. Since we are not professional writers, this was quite a daunting task, and Jean made it an absolute pleasure. We are eternally indebted.

Special thanks to PetsMart Superstores. There is no denying the fact that our association with this exciting, pet-loving company has the potential to help us grow until . . . until . . . we are a great big ol' biscuit-bakin' company. That has always been our dream, ever since we were cutting out our treats by hand around the kitchen table. Every associate at PetsMart, from the chairman of the board on down, has been nothing but 100 percent supportive, enthusiastic and positive. An extra-grateful pawshake to Ron Butler and Don Dorsey for honoring us by serving on our board of directors and for their **big-time** help, support and guidance. Also to Joe Bayless who so often makes time for us out of his busy days to help us think like a grrrowing company. **We only hope that we can give you back as much as you are giving us.** Thanks, PetsMart!

The Most Special Thanks of All to: The World's Greatest Employees, all of our partners here at Three Dog Bakery. So many of you came to work here because you truly believe in the concept and what we are trying to accomplish. Many of you even took pay cuts to come work for us! Besides taking grrrrreat pride in everything you do, you constantly amaze us by going beyond the call of duty again and again. We are blessed with the kind of staff that jumps right in and gets the job done, no matter what it takes. You have frozen through the coldest winters and sweated through the hottest of summers. All of your efforts are terrifically appreciated.

Our hats are off to you, the people who make it all happen:

VICE PRESIDENT OF MARKETING
Evan Wooton
VICE PRESIDENT OF FINANCE
Terri Valentine
VICE PRESIDENT OF OPERATIONS
Rocky Valentine
ASSISTANT CORPORATE SECRETARY
Mary Jane Porter

117

NATIONAL ACCOUNTS MANAGER/SAN DIEGO MARKET MANAGER
John Escalada
PURCHASING MANAGER
Sharon Jordan
CUSTOMER SERVICE DIRECTOR
Laura Dunaway
MANUFACTURING MANAGER
Troy Alldaffer
PRODUCTION SUPERVISOR (DAYSIDE)
Lindsey Carter
PRODUCTION SUPERVISOR (NIGHTSIDE)
Ngullen (William) Torres
EXECUTIVE PASTRY CHEF
Patricia Berlau
COMMISSARY CHEF
Laura Burbaugh
PASTRY CHEFS
Sharon Bilharz, Patsy Edelmann, Mark Marshall, Patty Martin,
Jackie Martino
FINISHING DECORATORS
Katia Hernandez, Sally McMillan, Christina Tejada
RETAIL SALES MANAGER
Sandy Brown
DISTRIBUTION MANAGER
Jeff Schwartz
DISTRIBUTION PROCESSORS
John Dix, Manuel Estrada, Nam Ho, Cuong La, Alfonso Rivera, John Tejada
PACKAGING SUPERVISOR (DAYSIDE)
Sofia Marin
PACKAGING SUPERVISOR (NIGHTSIDE)
Vivian Torres
SPECIAL PROJECTS
Greg Wilson
RECEPTIONIST
Rosemary Carney

PACKAGING SPECIALISTS

Linda Aguilar, Alma Arzate, Maria Chavira, Gisela Estevez, Yvonne Garcia, Bach Le, Trang Luu, Rita Montano, Bich Nguyen, Dam Nguyen, Huong Nguyen, Thao Nguyen, Mayra Rivera, Lan Tran, Thu Tran

PRODUCTION TECHNICIANS

Oscar Brene, Oscar Chavira, Francisco Estrada, Leonardo Estrada, Alfredo Fuentes, Silvia Gonzales, David Gorrita, Christine Hardy, Robert Hernandez, Phong Huynh, Miguel Niera, Mike Neira, Thanh Nguyen, Michael Sumstine, Samuel Torres, Yoel Torres

SALES

Luis Avila, Mercedes Avila, Felicity Benton, Jenifer Doleshal, Connie Duvic, Lyla Galvan, Karen Hight, Tara Ingalls, Jennifer Jasa, Brandee Kochan, Susi Mike, Amy Modlin, Heather Rubio, Nancy Villafañe

A very warm and special thanks to Mrs. Phyllis Dokken (aka Grammy) for adopting all of us and fattening us up with her very yummy homemade bakery treats. She bakes the way only a North Dakota grand- mother can. The world would be a lot better place if everyone shared their goodies the way Grammy does. **Thanks, Grammy, on behalf of the whole crew!** (And that definitely includes Dottie, Sarah and Gracie!)

Hey! If you're traveling through Kansas City, please come give us a sniff! Stop by our bakery at 612 W. 48th St., on the Country Club Plaza. Our phone number is (816) 753-DOGS. We're open seven days a week, and we'd love to meet you!

For a free (yes, free) Three Dog Bakery Dogalog® (no cat-alogs for us!), please drop us a line at:

Three Dog Bakery
1706 Holmes St.
Kansas City, MO   64108

Or call us toll free at:
(800) 4-TREATS
and we'll send one right out.

For all you cyberheads, we urge you to contact us at our web site:
http://www.threedog.com

We hope to hear from you!

Rrrrecipe Index

From the Authors

Who Says Dreams Don't Come True?

On behalf of everyone here at Three Dog Bakery, we'd like to say **THANKS AGAIN** for buying our book. We hope that you found our short "tail" interesting, entertaining – hopefully even inspirational.

Thank you for helping us to realize some of our dreams. Believe us when we tell you that if we can achieve our dreams, so can you. Believe powerfully in yourself, believe powerfully in all of your dreams, work hard, keep your paws planted firmly on the ground and sniff out new opportunities. Remember to wag your tail as often as possible – and hey! no growling!

Dan • Mark

GRacie   SaRah   Dottie